EMBATTLED LAND

Beata Lipman is a Jewish feminist, a refugee from Germany, who grew up in South Africa where she lived and worked for 30 years. She now lives in Wales and works as an independent television producer. Beata Lipman is the author of *We Make Freedom: Women in South Africa* (Pandora Press, 1984; rpt 1986).

ISRAEL: THE EMBATTLED LAND

JEWISH AND PALESTINIAN WOMEN TALK ABOUT THEIR LIVES

by Beata Lipman

Sally
Please share these
troubled thoughts!
Beata
April 5 1989.

PANDORA

London, Sydney, Wellington

First published by Pandora Press, an imprint of the
trade division of Unwin Hyman Limited, in 1988

Set in 10 on 11½ pt Sabon
by Columns of Reading
and printed in Great Britain
by The Guernsey Press Co. Ltd.
Guernsey, Channel Islands

Unwin Hyman Limited
15–17 Broadwick Street
London W1V 1FP

Allen & Unwin Australia Pty Ltd.
8 Napier Street, North Sydney, NSW 2060, Australia

Allen & Unwin New Zealand Pty Ltd,
with the Port Nicholson Press
60 Cambridge Terrace, Wellington, New Zealand

British Library Cataloging in Publication Data
Lipman, Beata
Israel: the embattled land: Jewish and Palestinian
women talk about their lives.
1. Israel. Society. Role of women
I. Title
305.4'2'095694

ISBN 08635–8286–9

CONTENTS

ILLUSTRATIONS

INTERVIEWEES

1 **HEBRON AND THE WEST BANK**
Geula Cohen
Shoshana Mageni
Miriam Levinger
Shifra Blass
Judy Loewe
2nd Lt Dennis Allon
Zoher

2 **THE ARMY AND MILITARISM**
Alice Shalvi
Netiva Ben Yehuda
Tamar Livney
Dalia Elkana
Col. Amira Dotan
Dana Arieli
Girls at Ulpan Akiva
Irene Hirschmann
Carmit Gie

3 **JERUSALEM THE GOLDEN**
Miriam Halevi
Shulamit Berger
Zahera Kamal
Mary Khass
Netiva Ben Yehuda
Ora

CHRONOLOGY

ISRAEL, WAR AND THE GROWTH OF ITS TERRITORIES
(see map, p. 4)

May 1948	Declaration of the State of Israel by United Nations. Attacked by five Arab armies, Israel successful in making territorial gains from UN partition plan.
1956	Suez campaign against Egypt in cooperation with France and Britain.
1967	Six Day War – massive territorial gains.
1973	Yom Kippur War. Attacked by Egypt and Syria. Israel handed Sinai back to Egypt after Camp David agreement in 1982.

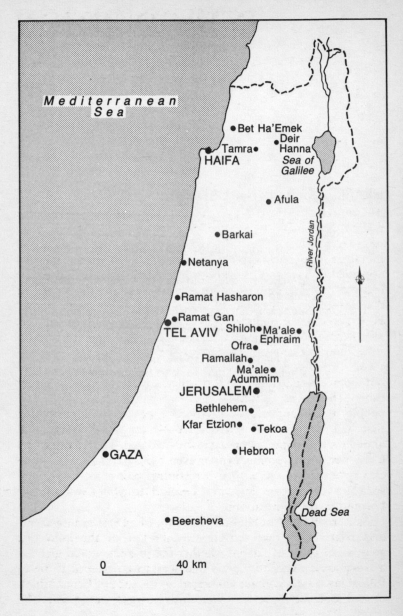

Map 1 Places mentioned in the text

INTRODUCTION

Why go to Israel? The pressure to visit, to look and see, and to use my journalistic skill to try and elicit something of the quality of women's lives there was challenging. I wanted to go on that journey of exploration, but when I looked at the literature one remarkable fact was instantly clear: no one appeared to have spoken to both Jewish and Arab women. The analyses to be studied were about one or the other. I determined to at least attempt both, even if not with parity. How perceive the quality of one person's life if not in contrast with others? And that meant different political perspectives too, from the most rabid of nationalists and the ultra-Orthodox to those who seek a secular society and a left-wing slant. I could not ignore one nation or the other, whatever people might think. There was a strong sense, even before I travelled, that people would approve or disapprove of me – not something that had bothered me when I set off for South Africa and another set of taped interviews with women. Here I thought I knew why – eyes on me, firm or even a bit glaring, saying quite clearly 'either you're with us or you're against us – and what sort of a Jew are you, anyway?' I would do what I wanted, but I would move with caution.

As a small child in Hitler's Germany I had lost grandparents and relatives in that terrible travail – I'm of the holocaust generation and I wondered whether the journey would give me a fresh sense of identity. The best way to go seemed to be to follow my nose – contact women in all the groups I could think of and look for those who were interesting. I would travel by

1

bus as much as possible, and not rely too much on family or friends. Would a proper picture emerge that way? What you see depends on where you look, to some extent.

I found a world where men have to be macho, competitive and tough. And women? On a bus ride between Beersheva and Jerusalem I sat next to a young woman in uniform on her way home for a weekend off from her Army duties in Dhahariya. It was only half past eight in the morning as she slung her rifle on board as though it were just another handbag, but she looked exhausted and tense. The commentator Amos Elon has spoken of the moral agony, the political failure and the economic muddle of a nation demoralised and divided against itself as never before in its forty years of life . . . a bit unfair, perhaps, to load all that on to this young Israeli Sabra,[1] but she found nothing to be joyful about on the West Bank that morning. Before I met Galit the decision had already been taken that the interviews would be mainly with women, and from a feminist perspective (and in spite of the political and traditional blocks I was finding in establishing contact with Arab women), but she helped me see it even more clearly. In a land where women sit at the bottom of the pile, where a military life, religious custom and current practice all contribute to their continuing oppression, I did want to salute their courage and their spirit in spite of all.

Since 1948 the lives of all who live in Israel and its surrounding territories have been continually warped and changed by war. With hardly a lull in the tension, the Israeli Defence Force needs to use the skills and resources of all but the most Orthodox young Jewish men for three years of their lives on a fulltime basis and those of young Jewish women for two. Arabs – except some Druze and Bedouin men – do not serve, but their lives, too, are profoundly affected by the ubiquitous military presence at home and across the border. War and its anxieties, its successes and losses and despair, have created bitterness and hatred although among many of the Jews who came to Israel from other Middle Eastern countries – the

1 Those born in Israel are known as Sabras, or prickly pears.

Sephardi – the feelings were already endemic because of old persecutions and segregation.

War, and the military society it has engendered in Israel, has not been good for those women who came to settle there because they believed in equality for their sex as well as a new home for Jews. It has not been entirely bad for those young Arab women who today pursue demands for their own liberation and that of their countrymen. Paradoxically, although they feel suppressed by Israeli law and Muslim tradition, they have been able to assert themselves more strongly – especially in their own homes – than young Arab women in other parts of the Middle East. Among Jewish families (and there are not many single women over the age of 25) war has reinforced the traditional roles forged by custom and religion: women are expected to be docile, supportive and to function mainly in the home while their husbands and partners spend weeks away each year on military service. Contemporary ideas of sharing childcare and domestic work, nascent in Western countries, have had even less impact here; it has even been suggested that a feminist consciousness poses a danger to continuing military effort.

Arab women, who are also supported (and controlled) in strong family groupings, are going out to work for the first time in their lives in factories, hospitals and service industries. Many of them have lost family land; thousands live in the refugee camps of Gaza and the West Bank. War and its economic and political aftermath have been stronger in the development of their new work roles than Muslim tradition and a private and domestic life.

War and conquest for the Israelis has entailed the reinforcing of gains, the need to buttress new frontiers: that has involved private citizens as directly as the Army. In Israel, the kibbutz has been an agricultural cooperative but also, frequently, a key outpost in new territory. On the West Bank and the Golan, new settlements have strategic use just as much as the kibbutzim had within Israel before and after 1948. Women, who came to Israel because they cared as much about egalitarian principles as for a promised land of Jewish independence, away from the

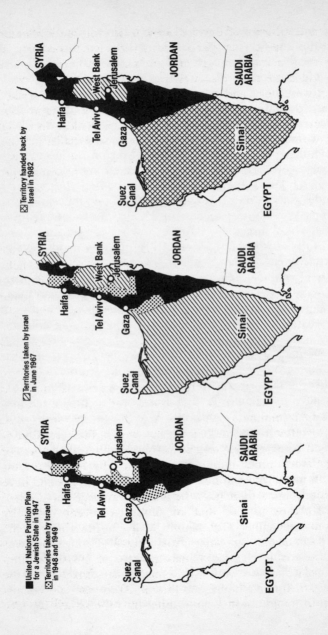

Map 2 The changing borders of Israel, 1947–1967

■ United Nations Partition Plan for a Jewish State in 1947

▨ Territories taken by Israel in 1948 and 1949

▨ Territories taken by Israel in June 1967

⊠ Territory handed back by Israel in 1982

ghettos and miseries of Europe, went to live on the kibbutzim in their thousands. They discovered that the excuses of war, as well as their lack of strength and endurance in heavy physical work, added to their disconcerting loss of continuity while children were born and reared, meant that they were pushed back into the interior, domestic frontier. The kibbutzim have documented the difference between egalitarian ideal and lived reality; women come off second best in these socialist havens, as elsewhere.

Yet among some of the other settlements matters are more paradoxical. The extremist Right group, Gush Emunim (the Bloc of the Faithful), who began settling the West Bank – initially against official Israeli policy – because they believe that all the land mentioned in the Old Testament belongs, as of theistic right, to the Jewish people, have among them effective and powerful women settlers. According to their own beliefs, these Orthodox women ought to be docile, but the frontiers mentality, the difficulties and stresses of pioneering, of living with a gun continually to hand, have made them too strong to be put away into a neat Scriptural box.

Many of the Arab women I met in Israel, the West Bank and Gaza also do not conform to meek standards. The war, for them, has been lost: but their demand for new political rights is linked with a need for self-fulfilment and personal dignity at a fresh level of independence. As women, they suffer discrimination in their community and they meet daily discrimination at work, in welfare rights and education, even in their freedom of movement. Arab women, except for those who are members of the large Israeli trades union federation, the Histadrut, earn less than Arab men. They, in their turn, earn lower wages and have larger family units than Jews, so that the average standard of living of Arabs is half that of Jews. (A recent move by education campaigner Ora Namir M.K. in the Knesset, the Israeli Parliament, for compulsory nursery education was defeated, she said, because 'Ninety percent of Jewish children already get it: success would have meant its extension, for the first time, to Arab children.' In addition, Arab men and women who live in Israel are not conscripted into the Israeli Defence

Force, although some Bedouin and Druze do join up on a voluntary basis. As Army service affects the level of benefits received by the family as a whole, welfare for Arabs within Israel is considerably less than that received by Jewish Israelis.)

And if Arabs are discriminated against in Israel today, many of the Jewish refugees who came there in the huge deluge of the early 1950s from Yemen, Iran, Morocco and elsewhere came from a life where Jewish schools were often closed, agriculture or the owning of land forbidden and their domain confined to a ghetto. Tziona, whose testimony appears later, had only three years of schooling; Miriam from Yemen had none. The Jews from the East, the Sephardi, today greatly outnumber the Ashkenazi or Western Jews who brought Western liberal traditions and democratic values to a Palestine where they were the first Jewish immigrants.

It was the predominantly Ashkenazi party, Mapai, that formed the first Labour government under David Ben-Gurion after the declaration of the State in May 1948. Labour held power in the Knesset, forming coalitions whenever necessary with smaller religious parties, and also through their dominance in the Histadrut, a unique trades union federation that owns its own industries (including a profitable and burgeoning arms industry) and enrols 90 per cent of the population in its sick fund, Kupat Holim. Today labour (now the Ma'arach) can be in government only in a major coalition with the Right because over the years its dominance, inside and outside the Knesset, has become eroded by the growth of Sephardi support for the Likud, a right-wing group that formed its first government in 1977 under the premiership of Menachim Begin. (In the struggles of 1947 and 1948, Begin had led the terrorist group Irgun Zvai Leumi that claimed responsibility for the bomb attack against the British, at the King David hotel in Jerusalem.)

The 120-seat Knesset has only 10 women members. Some of the smaller parties are the small Citizens Rights Movement led by Shulamit Aloni and two groups to the right of Likud – Tehiya (Renaissance), also with a woman leader, Geula Cohen, and the overtly racist Kach, whose Knesset member Rabbi Meir

Kahane calls for the forcible removal of Arabs from Israel and the West Bank. (He and Begin, and most of today's Likud's activists, share the belief that only 'Greater Israel' – to include all the present militarily administered West Bank and Gaza – will do as a final home.) A few small religious groupings handle power beyond any relation to their size because they are continually wooed by the larger parties when they seek to establish a government; linked with the power of the rabbinate, this has affected legislation that concerns women in a reactionary and retrogressive way.

Much has been made of Israel's universal suffrage and the lack of such political rights in other Middle Eastern countries, but the liberal left feels that democracy to be severely endangered. In a 1986 survey done by Professor Sami Smoocha of Haifa University, 58 per cent of all those Jews questioned did not trust Israel's 700,000 Arabs and a popular 'solution' was that they should be expelled. Many believed Arabs should lose the right to vote for an Israeli Parliament and a large majority felt that Jews who supported the idea of an independent Palestinian state on the West Bank should also lose that privilege.

The rights of democracy and those conveyed by the fundamental constitutional right of all Jews to come to Israel and have immediate citizenship (the Law of Return) are, in the eyes of many Arab observers, unjustly linked. Until 1967 Arabs who were away from their own homes during the upheavals of 1948 lost their land, but not the right to stay, or to vote. Since 1967 they have been unable to return at all. Mary Khass, who grew up in Haifa and now works as an administrator in Gaza, is angry about the different treatment of Arab and Jew: 'It's discrimination of the worst kind. It makes a mockery of the Knesset and its democratic procedures, and of the Declaration of Independence that says all citizens will have equal rights without distinction of race or creed.' That discrimination is also reflected in daily life: in 1986 the Prime Minister, then Shimon Peres, told the Knesset that Arab local authorities received only 30 per cent of the subvention to Jewish towns and cities. He said State funds were not invested in industry or sewage systems in Arab areas and that education was 'in very bad shape'. Forty years of war and struggle between Arab and Jew have had prolific consequences.

A direct result of the hostility and pressure is that women are encouraged to have as many children as possible. Be fruitful and multiply, which was an injunction to have a boy and a girl, is now taken as encouragement to have a new baby every year. Among Orthodox Jews contraception is against the law and – although it is not illegal – contraceptive advice is difficult to obtain. But in spite of Orthodoxy (and if you walk along any tree-lined avenue in Jerusalem you will see pregnant young women by the score) the Arab population is growing more rapidly. There too it is a matter of political honour, of settling old scores and making a statement about the future. In 1984 there were 78,600 Arab births and 74,350 Jewish ones. There are more than 2 million Arabs in the three territories and 3½ million Jews, but it is the rate of growth that worries or interests the population statisticians and the politicians: 45 per cent for Jews over twenty years, 72 per cent for the Arabs. The forecast is for parity between the two peoples by AD 2000 – and that forecast has helped fan racist flames and fears.

During my journeying in Israel and the West Bank I was invited to meet an Arab family at Tamra, in Galilee. Which would be the best way to travel there from Jerusalem? The bus routes favoured the coastal plain, and as I tried to determine a different, inland way through the Samarian hills I saw there was no demarcation, no 'Green Line' to show where Israel ended and the West Bank began. All three maps in my possession (and not all of them bought in Israel) were the same: there were no border markings on any of them. Everyone spoke of the line with detailed exactness, house to house, village to village, tree to rock cache. But formally, on paper, it did not appear to exist.

Again, after the Tamra visit I travelled with Steve Leibowitz of the government-sponsored briefing organisation, Diplomatic Services. His descriptions were graphic – the Jordanian guns were trained on us here; this is where our people were slaughtered in 1948; from here we must command the heights for ever. Again we spun in and out of the West Bank without clarification. Was Greater Israel a lived reality that we outsiders knew nothing of? When I drove to Gaza I took my place in a queue of cars waiting to enter the Strip at an Army checkpoint, only to be asked whether I had lost my way ... all the other Jews were driving through without hindrance: it was a change of territory, this time defined by the colour of the car numberplate. Paradoxically, the area was also defined by fear: if you had any sense, I was told, you would certainly not drive there on your own or catch a bus that way if there was an alternative route. Behind the glass walls lay a land to be cherished, but it was full of dangerous strangers.

In Tamra I was met with friendly courtesy by Rhodina and Ali. At bedtime they insisted I use their room and they joined their two young children on the sleeping mats in the adjacent bedroom. Rhodina does not go out to work but both of them helped in the preparation of the next morning's meal. I was the first Jewish visitor they had ever entertained, although they have lived all their lives in Israel. When I met the author Netiva Ben Yehuda a few days later, she lamented that there was so little contact between Arab and Jew: 'We live in two closed tunnels. We don't see them, they don't see us. We live side by side in ignorance of each other.'

Netiva Ben Yehuda is among the liberal women I met – Arab and Jew – who do try to meet those from the other side, even if only sporadically. Frequently their belief in liberation for women is conjoined with political radicalism. Those most hostile to the powerful concepts connected with women's rights and opportunities, most secure in a niche that happily contains children, religion and the kitchen, are also the most devout. Often, too, they stand on the political right and seemed most ready to dispose of a third of the population of Greater Israel altogether. I went to an open air meeting of the Women's Work Committee with some of the Arab radicals I had met, and was not surprised to find a large police presence muscling in on proceedings. But of the Jewish radicals, Esther Elliam of the Citizens Rights Movement – which stands for human rights for all – says that it is not rights, political or feminist, that concern people; it's the daily struggle for survival.

That affects everyone. With so much of the budget going to defence, and a further quarter to pay off the interest on loans, welfare is tight and unemployment continues to grow. The health service, Kupat Holim, has had its funds slashed. Yet the Israeli Army remains the largest, per head of population, of any country that publishes its figures – ten times more than West Germany and greater, pro rata, than the United States during the holocaust years of the Second World War. Ninety-six per cent of the white-collar jobs are taken by Jewish men and women, leaving the growing number of graduate Arabs with only labouring jobs to apply for. The other alternative for Arabs, and for many years the traditional route to skilled and well-paid work, was to work in the Gulf countries. There the changing oil situation has meant that thousands have returned home to unemployment.

Middle-class Arab women are entering 'women's work' in growing numbers – as teachers, administrators, nurses and health visitors. Many are hairdressers or dressmakers; whatever their work or status, those who live away from the parental home if they are not married are rare. One per cent of the people of Israel earn 11½ per cent of its income but women take home only 14 per cent of the overall total, in spite of the fact that those working far exceed that figure.

My journeying led to Yad Vashem, the holocaust museum near Jerusalem where there are long lists of those who died in the concentration camps of Germany and Poland during the Second World War. My grandfather, Heinrich Hirschmann, had been sent to Dachau when he was 70; there he had died, like so many others, I was looking for a name, the affirmation of his being. The German explosion had been, for me, the experience of a large, well-knit family scattered to the threadbare winds and lost, I felt, in America, in Palestine, in Britain. My parents tried to keep in touch with brothers, sisters, uncles and aunts. I remembered how they had sent small sums here, warm letters there, as they struggled to pay their own bills.

We were uprooted, frightened, lost. A grandmother in Leipzig wrote to us all — someone else had an exit visa; a grandchild had started school in the States: she tried to act as the fulcrum of a tiny diaspora. One day, in November 1938 she could bear the Nazi's methods no longer. She wrote a last note in her spidery writing and then she switched on the gas . . . now, in Israel, the holocaust was vivid reality. From the time that the Romans had taken Jerusalem until that war, Jews had placed a far greater emphasis on pacifism than military might. They had abjured power based on the gun, but now, for forty years, it had been at the centre of almost every struggle. The resulting pressure has been overwhelming.

The struggle to survive, to win every war, to maintain and extend the borders, has taken a major and enervating toll. This is a raw, angry and touchy society where the arguments betwcen Sephardi Jew and Ashkenazi Jew, between Orthodoxy and agnosticism are, at times, as severe and violent as any between Arab and Jew: where the ultra-Orthodox burn down half Jerusalem's bus shelters to remove the skimpily dressed womcn on advertisements and their opponents have burnt a synagogue and defaced holy books. Racism and brutality grow, and among high school students support for Mcir Kahane and Kach has never been higher. I had set off on an enterprise where I felt decimated, at times, by a great deal more than the unaccustomed heat of a Middle Eastern high summer.

• •

CHAPTER 1

HEBRON AND
THE WEST BANK

A Friday, and Muslims are being called to prayer on the public address system in Hebron's marketplace. We worry about more prosaic matters: where to park the hire car with its bold yellow number plates – for safety, it ought not be left too far away from the small Jewish enclave behind the shops and the fruit and veg stalls. There, sullen young Israeli soldiers are on guard all the time; further up the incline of the main square, next to the ancient Muslim cemetery, with its tombs like upturned teacups without handles, I feel less comfortable. The stares of the young Arab men, and of the boys kicking a ball nearby, are bold and hostile.

Never travel alone on the West Bank, I had been told over and over again. But in the course of their daily lives many women who have chosen to live there do it all the time, often with a gun on the car seat beside them. One of the women I had come to interview, Shifra Blass, had driven alone for years: she and her colleagues had defied government policy and gone, illegally, to establish the first Jewish settlement on the West Bank at Ofra, and eventually the same – Labour – government gave the settlers arms to defend themselves in the very territory they were committed to returning, at least in part, to local Arabs.

Here in Hebron, with its large Arab population, the government had also said No to settlement but Jews, obdurately believing that each place mentioned in the Old Testament, the Torah, belonged to Israel by biblical precedent, had, provocatively, stayed on, demanding the Army's protection. They were a few dozen among thousands of Arabs, living rough where necessary. Had not King David make Hebron the capital of his kingdom before he conquered Jerusalem? They felt it a holy duty to remain.

Neri – born in Israel, passionate, left-wing and stationed in Hebron during his Army service – had volunteered to accompany me. His friend Dana would take pictures.

It is oppressively hot. I park at the bottom of the incline and we walk past aubergine and water melon, strangely shaped tomatoes and cucumber. The public address system booms on. Behind the market, past a fence with barbed wire and the dour, armed soldiers there are tiny, twisted alleys, stone arches, staircases going nowhere and the old stone houses, mostly derelict, that had housed the Jewish community until the massacre in 1929. Massacre or no, and in spite of bible history, the action to return is provocative; the tension and the smell of hate, on both sides, overpowering.

Rachel Levy, who lives with her husband and ten children in Hadassah House, bases her life on this return to 'her' land and that of her sons. (The four daughters, helping with the preparation for the Sabbath meal that evening, are not mentioned during our discussion.) She arrived in the first group of settlers soon after the war in 1967 that brought the West Bank under Israeli Army control, under the leadership of Rabbi Moshe Levinger and his wife Miriam. Rachel is allowed to go shopping in the marketplace by the Israeli soldiers, but Levinger is stopped. Neri says it is because the soldiers fear he will deliberately be aggressive, seeking a knifing, a curfew, so that his group can grab a few more rooms, another house, some feet of precious space from local Arabs. I asked Rachel to talk about her life and beliefs on tape, but she insists, instead that I speak to the Levingers.

Another good friend of Miriam and Moshe Levinger is Rafael Eytan, formerly of the Tehiya Party. Now a member of the Knesset, Eytan was the Army's chief of staff during the war in Lebanon – when he became known for calling Arabs 'cockroaches in a bottle'. His approach to the situation in Hebron is 'We must vary our responses. In Tunis we bombed them . . .

what we did with an F15 in Tunis can be done in Hebron with an Uzi. If you know of a terrorist here, go and kill him in his bed.' (Many Uzi submachine guns leased from the police are in private hands.)

Geula Cohen is the leader of Tehiya in the Knesset. During my stay she was one of a small group that squatted on mattresses in another old house in Hebron in defiance of a government ban on any further Jewish settlement in the town. 'It's shameful,' she says, 'A Jew can buy property anywhere in the world except in Hebron.' Yet the well-documented details show that since the 1967 takeover, Jews have acquired more than 50 per cent of the Arab land of the West Bank.

Mrs Cohen has been a political activist since 1947. She was active in the Stern Gang, the Lechi.

In 1948 I was in the Army, but not used for combat because I was married. But I was the broadcaster for the Stern group, a very extreme branch of the underground that was involved with the assassination of Count Bernadotte. I made a special broadcast.[1] I spoke about Bernadotte and his plans, and how much his policies would have hurt the Jews, especially in Jerusalem: the worst was his plan for the internationalisation of the city.[2] Even now, because of his plan, the embassies are in Tel Aviv and the world does not recognise Jerusalem as our capital. (She was responsible for the Knesset Bill in 1981 that declared Jerusalem the eternal capital of Israel.)

Today Geula Cohen says she does not believe in violence.

For me the activity in the Knesset is not academic but a

---

1 Count Folke Bernadotte, a member of the Swedish royal family, was appointed United Nations mediator in Israel in May, 1948, to watch over the birth of the new nation. On September 17, as he arrived in Jerusalem to inspect a new headquarters building, he was ambushed and killed by the Stern Gang, who said ... 'all United Nations observers in Palestine are members of foreign occupation forces which have no right to be in our territory'.
2 Count Bernadotte had proposed that Jerusalem should be administered on an international basis.

continuation of my struggle for my people and my country, which began when I was sixteen years old and joined the underground. Behind my civilian dress it is as though I am still in khaki. If you ask me what makes a real Jew: to be a Jew is to be a fighter.

Today the head of the arrow, the real pioneers, are Gush Emunim[3] because they are continuing the enterprise of Zionism, which is to go on settling Eretz (the land) Israel. It's like the struggle we had before 1948, to establish the land against a foreign government: now, to settle Judea and Samaria on the West Bank we are fighting our own Zionist government. Really, saying there's no money is only an excuse; the Labour Party are against the new settlements because they want a territorial compromise.

I want to see Israeli sovereignty in Judea and Samaria, the territory as an organic part of the State of Israel: it is the heart of our historic land. The Arabs there are citizens of Jordan and we are not going to force them to be Israeli citizens. They can still be Jordanians, or if they want to leave they can leave.

If one or two, or one thousand, two thousand or ten thousand wish to be Israeli citizens it will be on private conditions. They will ask, each one of them, and we will debate any request personally . . . and not only because they are citizens of a state like Jordan which was an enemy to us, and tried three times to destroy us.[4] Not only because of that; if I go to the States and I want to be a citizen, automatically I'll be one? No, I have to be there five years, and I have to be tested in many ways – my loyalty to the State should be tested. It's the same thing here only much more so, because many of the Arabs support the PLO, the enemy of Israel. So we will see about each request.

I myself was not a terrorist. I was a freedom fighter for my

3 Gush Emunim, the 'bloc of the faithful', take the Old Testament literally: the commandment to 'possess the land and conquer it' is seen as final and absolute.
4 Geula Cohen is referring to the three major wars – 1948, 1967 and 1973 – with various Arab armies.

country, as every fighter is. I fought against foreign governments, against imperialism which came here for its own interest. I never was a terrorist – I was a freedom fighter. The young Jewish terrorists today are fighting against illegal people: this is our home and our land and it was never theirs. Never in history was there a Palestinian state. They want one now and whoever helps them will give them part of *our* land.

I think I became a freedom fighter because my mother was an example for me, even though she was at home. She had ten children, but all the time she helped others; the door was open to help everyone in the streets. She taught me to give everything I can to help my people. In her own way she was a fighter too; and while my father prayed for the redemption of Israel, in the synagogue in Yemen, he too was working for Israel.

I believe in the women of Israel, I believe they are fighters; a woman is a political person. She has many of the abilities and qualities needed in fight; she is brave. She smells the risks to the lives that she gives birth to from her womb and she is more sensitive to the dangers in life than a man. You see such women in Gush Emunim: they are either breast-feeding or their belly is in front of their body because they are pregnant. They bear many children and still they are in the first line of struggle in the settlements. I see them on the roof with a gun in their hand, fighting in the hills and on the mountains, one hand with their husband, one with their children.

Even in the time before the State of Israel was law, even before I was born, the women were already in my underground, in the Stern gang and the other groups that existed. Their contribution was not trivial; it was not only to help the boys but to fight with the boys. Today the women in Ofra and the other Gush Emunim settlements are still doing much more than any woman in Tel Aviv and Haifa. They are not only risking their own life . . . a mother who is sending her children to school through Arab villages, her heart is dying three times a day.

But not everyone can be a pioneer – in all the wars and all

the sagas the pioneers are few. It needs a special character to be idealistic twenty-four hours a day.

I am not for Kahane's policy of expelling all the Arabs from Judea and Samaria. I want to expel the PLO leaders, the PLO activists, the terrorists who don't want to recognise the Jewish Zionist State of Israel. Everyone who accepts the sovereignty of the Jewish Zionist State, not only in Israel but also in Judea and Samaria,[5] has a place in my heart – and everyone who does not and is fighting the fact has a place across the border.

KIRYAT ARBA

A few kilometres outside Hebron stands the contemporary Jewish town of Kiryat Arba, built by the same Labour government in the 1970s that had promised no settlements on the West Bank. It was built in the hope that the political embarrassment of action by Jewish squatters in Hebron would cease; instead, its existence is seen as yet another victory for the religious zealots who take the Torah literally, and who have so actively undermined every possibility of returning at least some of the West Bank to its Arab population of nearly a million people.

In 1985 Kiryat Arba's town council attracted a great deal of publicity by announcing that all its Arab employees would be fired – the gardeners, cleaners and garbage collectors. Arab investment in the area would be blocked, as well as any joint enterprise between Jew and Arab. The council has representatives of Meir Kahane's Kach party[6] on it to help force such initiatives, but the other council members – all men – gave full support. Again, biblical precept is used: the

5 Judea and Samaria are the biblical names given in Israel to the two parts of the West Bank – south and north of Jerusalem.
6 The Kach political party, although it only has one Knesset member (Rabbi Meir Kahane) overtly espouses racism and calls for the expulsion of all the Arabs who have political rights within Israel, as well as those who live in the West Bank and Gaza, where they hold none.

local development company calls on Deuteronomy, supported, they say, by the guidance of Israel's two chief rabbis. Kahane's party is committed to the expulsion of all the Arabs of Israel, the West Bank and Gaza from their homes and is adept at gaining publicity for itself whenever there's a killing or an action with racist overtones.

Shoshana Mageni also quotes from the Bible. A former American, she has lived in Hebron and Kiryat Arba for eight years with her husband, a coach operator who provided rides for her student group in Jerusalem. They have eight children and when we visited, at midday on a Friday, all except the youngest were at work to prepare for the Sabbath, when no work may be done. Shoshana left the cooking and the cleaning to sit on a low wall in the shade:

Oh, we *are* interested in keeping the Arabs here: they do the dirty work everywhere in Judea. We give them plenty of employment. I would be interested in finding an Arab town that employs Jews . . . we live close to them, day by day. But have you ever tried to do business with an Arab?

We will stay here, they can leave if they want. Our right to this land is historical, ever since Abraham bought a burial cave in Hebron five thousand years ago.
We will expand and take all this land for our own . . . we are making it fertile. God is not a racist; Arabs are getting the benefit from the fertility we have made. They can stay as residential aliens, like any other non-Jew who accepts the sovereignty of Israel, otherwise they'd overpower us in the Knesset – it would be like a knife in the back. We in Gush Emunim want them to accept the seven Mitzvot[7] as well: that would give us an assurance of basic moral standards.
The Jews in Jerusalem and Tel Aviv delude themselves if

7 The Mitzvot – an expanded form of the Ten Commandments – are the ethical standards drawn up for a resident stranger. Once they have been accepted by that person, respect and protection must be granted.

they think that if we were to give Hebron back to the Arabs they'd leave us in peace; what they really want is to rule the country and throw us into the sea. No, the only way to do it is to make them sign as aliens – otherwise they shouldn't get any welfare or protection of any kind. And if they threw one rock they'd be out! Let them advance in their own world – they'll not be the manager in my house. No one can require us to love our enemies.

I've got so many children because we accept the basic requirement: it's a Mitzvah[8] to be fruitful and multiply – in essence that means only one son and one daughter, but in the situation in Israel today it's important to have as many children as you can. We don't think eight is enough – let's hope we get to twelve!

Of course not everyone feels like we do. It is possible to use contraceptives, but only if the Rov and the doctor agree and if the husband gives his consent. I don't mind that it should be all men deciding . . . and the rabbis aren't all unsympathetic to us, either.

Later during my journey I met many Jewish women, originally from North Africa, Iraq, Syria or the Yemen, who were afraid to discuss contraception with husband or rabbi: they used cheap, and not so cheap, back street abortions as the very worst kind of prevention. In law, it is possible to have an abortion if one is under 17 or over 40, or if there is 'danger to of female humility and service within the home which have techniques under daily political and religious pressure among both Arab and Jew.

Shoshana, Miriam Levinger, Shifra Blass whom I was to meet later in Ofra, Rachel – all wore the appropriate garments of the Orthodox second sex, their hair hidden under a scarf and arms and legs covered, whatever the weather. Like Geula Cohen, they took an active part in shaping their own lives and were often forceful members of their community. The paradox of being deliberately excluded from all town councils with as

8 A commandment.

strong an Orthodox flavour as their own did not concern them, nor were they worried about their traditional roles as homemakers. As religious Jews they did not question the tenets of female humility and service within the home which have informed Jewish writing for centuries.

Miriam Levinger spoke for the Jewish women on the West Bank who are strongly Orthodox (as many as 80 per cent of the 80,000 who live there) when she said:

> In Judaism, a woman who has something to say can always do so without any formal involvement. In the elections, the women are simply left out of a ritual built round a gentile value. Democracy is non-Jewish and in my opinion has not proved itself sufficiently. Judaism has been around for thousands of years and democracy is merely a manipulative practice . . . it's only a tool, and certainly not a sacred value.

OFRA

At Ofra, also on the West Bank but to the north of Jerusalem, the dynamic, voluble Shifra Blass is a founder member. She is in the grip of a belief that provides her with enormous confidence for the daily strain of living among hostile people in a territory that she believes to be God-given to the Jews, but which a not insignificant section of Israelis think ought to be returned to the Palestinians.

> We came into a land inhabited by Arabs. We felt – how could anyone stop us? What law could they make to say a Jew can't live in Schrem, or near Shiloh? We found out there were laws, and we decided to circumvent them. How can the government of Israel discriminate against us as Jews? They are still enforcing Jordanian law . . . they adopted the rules, the international regulations relating to a foreign occupier, simply for expediency. They added, of course, Israeli military regulation and did away with some of the Jordanian law. But one they continued to administer was that Jews couldn't buy land here.

We felt there were loopholes: what if we came as American citizens, and didn't say which religion we were, but said: 'Here we are, we'd like to buy land' – couldn't we do something?

Couldn't we set up a company in Delaware: a land trading company from the United States? At one point my husband had a student who was taking lessons to convert to Judaism; he wasn't Jewish though. He said he would help us buy the land before the conversion: what could they do afterwards?

In 1979 the Knesset changed the law, and the minister of Defence was able to dispose of some land, like Ofra, which had been a military installation before Israel took over in 1967. From 1979 we could also start to buy land privately and today there are more than 50,000 Jews on the West Bank.

What is the mood and the feeling today? I certainly don't live in daily fear of our Arab neighbours. When we came I didn't feel any danger, our neighbours were quite nice to us and I didn't see any reason that any Arab would be upset at our being here if we didn't take anything from them. In fact I thought in very American terms: if you come and bring a little action into the area, you bring a little business, you bring a little life, people can only be happy with the development. This is the way the Zionists always came to Israel, they came and then the Arabs moved in and followed them exactly to where they were, because there were jobs and development . . .

We don't walk about with guns in our hands all the time. We are trained by the Army to use guns if necessary, but nobody counts on that.[9] It's done in the manner that the Army insists on, but nobody takes it too seriously . . . in order to use a gun well you have to have a lot of practice, and I wouldn't recommend to any woman that they really seriously try to take up arms to defend themselves. I would

9 Jewish women in Israel are expected to do a minimum of two years Army service when they finish school, although many do community service instead, arguing for it from a base of religious Orthodoxy. Arab women do not serve in the Israeli Defence Force.

not recommend it to any women who knows how to take a gun apart and put it together, and has learnt how to aim at a static target, which we all have to do . . . they would probably shoot their feet or their neighbours or something. You have to be really good at it, you have to practise and do drills the way men do.

Yet Shifra Blass never travels outside the settlement without a gun on the car seat by her side.

One of the roads leading to the settlement has had hand grenades placed there, and even on the perimeter fence there have been small bombs that have gone off, but thank God have not hurt anyone. That's the closest anyone has come to an actual settlement because terrorists prefer the weakest targets; that's why school buses are targets. But the community where people are at home all day – there's an image built up of us walking about there with guns and the terrorists don't want to tangle with us. That's why they go to crowded population centres, to the open air market on Wednesday, to a movie house. That's what they look for.

If you live in Israel, if you're a timorous type you have to overcome that because you have to realise that any place you are in the world, there's danger even if you stay in bed. What you have to do is – do what you want to do and balance out the risks. The statistics are generally in your favour in Israel – the terrorist events are lower than they are outside the country.

At the same time I think an Arab terrorist would not hesitate at this stage to plan and carry out, in cold blood, the most vicious attack on civilians in this country because there is no penalty that can deter him; no death penalty and not even a long gaol term. Just look at the terrorists who have been caught after the event, on the scene, red-handed – how many of them have been killed? You have a government that's supposed to enforce the law; if it did so people would be able to discriminate between criminals and Arabs, between terrorists and Arabs. That's why people are willing to accept Kahane as their safeguard: he wants them out.

He doesn't care whether you get them out nicely and pay them or whether you chase them, but he wants them out. If the government can't tell the difference between a terrorist and an Arab, because there's no harsh penalty for any terrorist, neither can Kahane and that's okay with us. He says get rid of everybody to protect us and the government says: Don't do anything. Because they don't protect us. I certainly prefer Kahane.

Today one in every seven of the Jewish population of Israel and the West Bank carry guns, from revolvers to submachine guns (the Uzi) and high velocity rifles. Israel has a thriving arms industry of its own and imports whatever else it needs.

Judy Loewe of the Jewish Agency[10] was chatty, quick, pleasant and informative. As our guide for the day trip to the West Bank from Jerusalem, she soon had thirty-six curious visitors settled. The air-conditioned coach left the Plaza Hotel for East Talpiot, one of the seven new neighbourhoods housing more than a hundred thousand people that have gradually ringed Jerusalem since the Israeli Defence Force took the eastern part of the city in 1967.

'When Jerusalem was liberated in the Six-Day War we were determined to turn it into a normal city, with enough residential areas and security to make it ours for ever,' Judy said. Part of making this new reality was by attracting fresh immigrants, or Olim. Judy was especially keen on those from North America, so we visited an absorption centre at Canada House. The large, modern stone building stood, like the apartments and houses about it, along the top of a hill – in fact all the neighbourhoods have been built as long rows of sturdy stone fortresses, there to defend the city 'forever'. Each home has a purpose-built bomb shelter. 'It's important we inhabit the

---

10 The Jewish Agency has been responsible for immigration and the buying and development of land in Israel before and after 1948. Today it is largely concerned with the growth of new settlements on the West Bank. Before the establishment of the new State in 1948 it was widely regarded as a provisional government and was responsible for collecting large sums of money annually from Diaspora Jews.

high places where we can look down on the lowlands: it's panoramic and strategic at the same time.'

At the centre rent is minimal. Most people stay for a year: there are Hebrew classes, a kindergarten, a laundromat, all the practical facilities to help ease the induction period while permanent settlement plans are made. Judy's phrase for it was, 'The women get used to the shops, the children to school, and the husband must buy an apartment.' Although only fifteen minutes from Jerusalem, housing costs are already at half the city's prices because of the high rate of government subsidy (and prices go down progressively if you're prepared to hang up your hat in ever newer settlements further into the West Bank).

The future lives of the women that I met at the absorption centre were, in their judgment, to be based on the care of their families and on having as many children as possible. Many had already decided that they wanted to settle on the West Bank, to help strengthen the concept of a 'Greater Israel' where no part of the former Jordanian territory would be returned either to that government or to the local inhabitants. 'What we have, we hold,' I was told. Only a few, who had arrived with large financial resources, planned to buy a home in Jerusalem, Haifa or Tel Aviv. The territory of the West Bank is only 80 miles long and 30 miles wide and official plans call for 200 Jewish settlements there by AD 2010. Could there really be any reality to the idea of peace talks, or even limited autonomy or self-determination for an area that was being settled so rapidly?

Judy Loewe had no doubts on the matter. She spoke with enthusiasm of the housing privileges given by the government to the men and women at the absorption centre – easy loans, outright grants, welfare benefits. At Tekoa, a brand new settlement further south that we visited later in the day, the land had been provided by the government, which had also paid for thirty houses. The seventy families on site had established a metal factory, a carpentry shop and a computer software business. Like the kibbutzim that had been established before the Israeli declaration of nationhood in 1948, these new outposts looked like the precursors of another territorial initiative. (After the war of 1948, 900,000 of Israel's 1.3 million Arabs had been displaced: more than a million Arabs live on the West Bank today.)

We drove on to Bethlehem, and to a place sacrosanct to religious Jews – Rachel's Tomb. Judy said the cunning old Jordanians had built a cemetery on three sides of the tomb during their control of the area between 1948 and 1967, as well as a road in front of it, so that no expansion and improvement of facilities could take place. But my neighbour on the coach, a New Yorker wearing a black skullcap, was pleased: 'The bigger the cemetery, the better: it means more dead Arabs.' He was cheerful in the midsummer heat. 'We must shoot them, of course,' talking of Arabs who threw stones at cars with the yellow number plates of Jews and tourists. He did not mention the orthodox Jews who threw stones as well – at the cars with yellow number plates that were driven by non-conformist Jews and disturbed their Sabbath, up and down the country, as I had seen in Kiryat Arba.

RAMALLAH

Next day it was hot enough to split the Jerusalem paving stones. I travelled north to Ramallah and a briefing from the civilian administrators of Israel's military government on the West Bank. Organiser Steve Leibowitz said, as we arrived in Ramallah: 'Administration means we can do what we please with the land here.' He waved an arm at the dry land and the white rock surrounding the Army camp. But Second Lieutenant Dennis Allon, who took the briefing, pointed out how fair the military administration was – they allowed the West Bank's citizens, who were Jordanians, to appeal against land expropriation in the Israeli Supreme Court.

By calling it an administrative area rather than occupied territory, the Israelis have avoided that part of the Geneva Convention which forbids individual or mass forcible transfers. In fact, Lt Allon said, a lot of people want to come in to the West Bank, not leave:

You're talking about conditions that are so ideal it's unbelievable. You're talking about an area where, within limits, you can speak out on anything you want. Economically – there's no unemployment in the area at all – zero unemployment. People want to come into the area; they can earn salaries far above those in the neighbouring countries. They earn Israeli salaries.

People can speak out: they can say pretty much what they want, except for, naturally, activities like terrorism, incitement or something like that. It's an idyllic situation and a lot of people try to get into this area. That's where the problems mostly emerge, rather than the reverse when we force people to leave. I'm still talking about an area that's under military rule – an administration that's trying to be as normal as possible in an abnormal situation. Given those constraints, there are going to be problems and conflicts.

Lt Allon believes living standards have jumped by leaps and bounds for everyone since 1967; but not more than in Israel.

Zoher also works in Ramallah. She had hoped to become a journalist and is very concerned about the living conditions of Arab women: she says the cost of living is high and salaries are low. Forty-five per cent of women on the West Bank are illiterate.

I once interviewed women workers in Israeli factories and in Arab factories. The owners make a deal with the fathers of the girls, to provide transport between the village and the factory, and to see they go straight home from work. The girls get the pay.

They have no chance to meet anyone in the cities or towns; they cannot join a union; they are strictly bound. But the paradox is that the fathers do let them go to work in a factory where there are men . . . in terms of the tradition even that shouldn't happen.

So economics are behind everything, because the fathers are taking most of the pay . . . he'll close his eyes and accept some things that have never been accepted before. The owners of the factories are also frightened of the trade unions from the political side, so it suits them very well to deal with the father and mother in this way.

We went once to visit a factory in the West Bank, to see the girls there, and I wanted to interview them. The owner knew me well, and he was embarrassed, but he told me he would never let me do an interview there. But women are joining the trade unions,[11] in spite of that . . . the work is being done in the villages instead. The work to persuade them to join the union, to demand their rights, to take up issues . . . 20 per cent of the members, today, are women instead of the 2 per cent three years ago.

I finished high school, and then went to work in the Gulf because I wanted to be independent of my father, my brothers . . . I wanted to pay my own University fees. So I went to work and studied at the same time. If I want to go from home for any work – to be a journalist, to write, to do what I believe would be good for my country, I need first to be liberated from my parents. They have to accept that I will be outside the home, and active.

Many parents refuse their daughters the right to be active; even if a parent lets a daughter go to University the parent is still in charge; and they do not let her choose her husband, or let her be a little independent in this. But because we have occupation in the West Bank and because we have troubles from the women and the men from the occupation, it has helped the women develop – more than in Lebanon, or Syria, or Egypt.

From the beginning my mother did help me! She had been a member of a women's self-help society for a long time, and she believes in the liberation of women. She treated us all the same at home, my brothers and me. She encouraged us to be

11 Arabs who live in Israel may join one of the trade unions affiliated to the Histadrut, the Jewish trade union federation that was formed even before the establishment of the State of Israel in 1948. Those on the West Bank and in Gaza are now starting to form their own unions but their bargaining and negotiating power is still slight.

independent, and to be proud of being girls. I had a chance here to work on a magazine, so I had to write the first subject about the women's liberation. It was a good start for me, and it encouraged me to continue.

I think the occupation is behind every difficulty we have on the West Bank. If I'm suffering from poverty, it means that economically the occupation is trying to damage the economy here. They refuse us permission to work, very often; and they won't let us build our own factories[12] . . . 90 per cent of the factories that have permission were already here before the occupation. The occupation is behind everything – our schools, our welfare: when I have a headache I say the occupation is behind my headache! The real reason behind my stretched nerves is the occupation . . . and the main thing now on the West Bank is the poverty.

Before 1967 we were under the Jordanian occupation here: today we will never accept to change the Israeli occupation for a second Jordanian occupation – King Hussein hasn't a hope! Ask anyone – any man, any woman, any boy who has never been political, and who has no connection with any side of any political organisation: they will tell you 'We hate Hussein as much as the present occupation. We know what the Jordanian government would do with us if they came back.'

I'm 30: I'm certain there'll be major changes in my life time . . . it doesn't matter when, after two years, after twenty years. We believe in our rights and we will have them. No one can finish off the Palestinian people, and as long as we exist we will fight for our rights. We will have what belongs to us, no matter how long it takes. We are not equal to the men in our struggle: we feel that if we want to be liberated we have to be equal with men in the front sides of life. The

12 Only seventeen factories on the West Bank employ more than twenty people. There are tanneries, flour mills, small cigarette and soap factories (the latter using olive oil), and a clothing industry. Recently plastic and chocolate manufacture has also begun.

women can't be at the same level as the men yet, because
tradition still holds us back.

If you want to step forward, some traditions are sending us
back four steps instead . . . I was trying to be a journalist, a
good journalist, but I was just as interested in my
appearance – after all, twenty-five years I'd been treated by
many people as though that was the only thing that
mattered. I was a beautiful girl and that was it. When I
became interested in my mind, and I found out that I wanted
to have a good mind as well as beauty, I learnt that it would
take a long time to change how I'd been raised. It will take us
time . . . I was thinking that I should be a good girl, think
well and study, maybe philosophy, whatever I want to
be – this I have only thought for five years. For twenty-five
years I was raised to be beautiful, to be a good mother and a
good wife.

My mother was a little bit stronger than my father.
Sometimes he didn't accept things, but because we were six
daughters as well as the sons, if we were all against him,
there was nothing he could do! He was forced to let us do
what we wanted. But it's not the same in the other families
round here . . . but there are many families here in Ramallah
where the mother is the leader of the house because the
father has gone to find work abroad. She works in the fields,
in the village, she works at home – most of the men are out
for a long time. It makes Palestinian women stronger than
other Arab women here.

Jews must teach their children to be racist, otherwise they
could not continue to behave towards us as they do. The
Jews are the best, they say. The religious idea that they are
the chosen people of God and the political side are linked.
They believe they bring civilisation, that Arabs are poor and
bad. Therefore they also believe we should be grateful and
not make a struggle with them. The Zionist is always putting
this idea in the mind of the Jewish people: to feel better than
the others, and to be strong together.

There are really too many differences between them:
they've even refused proper identity to the Ethiopians who

have come to Israel. I think the Palestinians, they aren't like this. Until now, we've been behind . . . we know we are weak now, and although we want our rights we are still weak. We know we are still the third world, and we need a lot to make progress.

Yes, of course there is hatred on both sides . . . but mostly it's Zionism I hate, not Jews. If one can make the connection with good Jews, as I have, then it becomes clear that it's the ideology, not the people. We hate the occupation, but we could live in peace if we got our rights. It's true there are some Jews I hate, but I haven't met them – Kahane, Begin, Geula Cohen: I hate them because of the ideas they hold for dealing with us.

I can visit Jewish women; I do, but usually there is no purpose for our contact. Our lives and our desires are on separate paths.

When Zoher drove me back to Jerusalem, she said she was familiar only with the 'Arab side' of the city, to the East, although she has lived in the area all her life. She didn't make it clear whether this was a matter of choice or the result of the apart and separate lives that Jews and Arabs live, but she was not eager to enter Jewish space and set me down a distance from my apartment. I felt the West Bank as metaphor as well as dusty reality; a metaphor for the past, when Jews had lived among Arabs on the land that is now Israel in similarly hostile conditions. The present, continually looking down the barrel of a gun, was no different and the image stretched in front of me, cold and seemingly endless. My journey of exploration had depressingly started.

CHAPTER 2

THE ARMY AND MILITARISM

The Israeli Defence Force is generally regarded as daring, resourceful and well organised by both detractors and proponents. As a country that has lived on a permanent trigger of war and invasion since 1948, Israel has developed a war machine that is implacable in defence, in attack, in surprise and surveillance. Without the successes of 1948, and again at Suez in 1956 and the Six-Day War of 1967, as well as the victory that followed for the Israelis after the Yom Kippur attack by Egypt and Syria in 1973, there would have been no continuing safety or even continued existence for its citizens. The latest war – Israel's invasion of Lebanon to gain the expulsion of the Palestine Liberation Organisation from the southern part of the country in 1982, and a subsequent three-year trial of attrition whose consequences are still being worked out in that sad country – brought to the surface, for the first time, major doubts within Israel about the perpetual militarism of the forty-year-old State, and a subsequent loss of morale.

I met no Israeli pacifists and no one, whatsoever their political view, who did not believe in the necessity of a system of defence. But the morass in Lebanon created, unusually, a questioning of values as well as tactics. After the massacres of Palestinians in South Lebanon, at Sabra and Shatilla in 1982, the largest demonstrations ever seen in Israeli streets took place as 300,000 Jewish men and women marched in protest, headed by the Peace Now movement (Shalom Akhshav). Mothers protested about the lengthy absence of sons at the front and formed their own protest lobbies; in all the action women – the

31

second sex in the Army but the prime bearers of all the extra burdens invoked by constant war and militarism – were at the forefront. They demanded an end to the war.

When it finally came, in the sumer of 1985, their burden, whether serving in the Army or at home, was no lighter. But they had shown an energy and resourcefulness that – according to the religious doctrines of Halacha – were not really in keeping with the modesty of the subdued position that the ages old law called for. As at other times of crisis in Israel, women had been emboldened to step beyond the narrowly defined roles of custom, practice and Jewish doctrine.

Professor Alice Shalvi discussed Jewish women's situation in the Army with me. She is head of an Orthodox school for girls and an energetic campaigner for women's rights.

One has to remember that there is no equality in the Army as far as duty and responsibility is concerned. Only the men are expected to do Army Reserve duty until they're 55. And no one except a few really extreme feminists would argue that women should go to the front and fight there, just as very, very few women here have gone to the extremes that radical feminists have explored in America, of wanting to abolish the family, or do away with marriage. Fighting at the front and abolishing the family – they fall into the same category: they're not really on the agenda. And I wonder whether the two approaches aren't part of the same philosophy.

So we have a society in which the family is seen as important and in which the men are away on Reserve for two months of the year; in which it is the men who are away in time of war – which has been only too frequent. That means that women perceive their function as being with the children at such times. So – given our security situation – women are the major childminders.

A military life is pushing women away from the opportunities for power sharing. It does it inevitably, unless one is prepared to abandon the family. The only way we could have equality here would be if we were to say 'Okay, no one will have children and the men and women will take equal responsibility for Army service.' It's not viable – and I wouldn't want it to be, either . . . that would be the death of our society.

Militarism has strengthened the traditional role and position of Jewish women in Israel; men help at home, but only when they're there, and the idea of actually re-thinking duties in any kind of fundamental way has never even arisen. Perhaps even more disturbing is Professor Shalvi's acceptance that war and its concomitant tensions are a permanent part of the Israeli scene.

In 1948 it *was* thought, in fact, that women would play a fully equal role in the Army organisations that existed before the declaration of the State of Israel. Netiva Ben Yehuda – today a prolific and popular author, and a lifelong proponent of a simple and colloquial written Hebrew – remembers when she joined the Palmach,[1] having just finished school, that she received exactly the same training as men:

> They invested a lot in us. I was an officer before the war
> started, of demolition, and reconnaissance, and topography:
> it was a lot of money and a lot of training. Till the war the
> men and women were 50:50. We were elected to be officers,
> or sergeants, or privates. Men and women, it depended on
> your strength and your competence, not your sex.
> At that time we admired the Arabs and imitated
> them . . . to us they were honest fighters, hospitable, noble. A
> man would talk slowly, he would control his face, he was
> beautiful: they had a kind of nobility for us. On the field he
> was not afraid of stones and thorns, he could smell the wind
> and its direction . . . then the war started: it was quite
> horrible in its cruelty and it had nothing to do with noble
> values.

1 The Palmach was the military organisation based on the kibbutzim that was one of the precursors of the regular Israeli Army. The egalitarian ideas of the kibbutz were also, initially, accepted for those serving and fighting in its ranks. Netiva Ben Yehuda has written about this time in her autobiograpical books *Between Calendars* and *Through the Binding Ropes*.

In fact what happened then had a great deal to do with the official order that soon came for women to leave the front line:

> Right at the start of that first war in 1948, when a platoon of the Palmach went on a field reconnaissance to the southern Negev, they were caught by Arabs on horseback with very long swords. Half managed to flee and the other half were caught . . . in a ritual killing they were slaughtered and their bodies mutilated. It's a law of the land here that mutilation always has something to do with sex: whenever you found the body of one of your comrades it was sexually mutilated.
>
> Imagination is nothing . . . no one can imagine the terrible sight. When we recover the bodies of the men, you can't imagine . . . people who saw it, they couldn't do anything for a week or two weeks until they woke up from the shock because you know, cutting off the genitals . . . and putting them in the brain or mouth, it's a terrible sight. They also mutilated one woman who was with those who were slaughtered, and immediately the order went out that we were not to fight any longer in the front lines. The order went down, down, down to the Palmach in the field to take all the women from the front lines, and all the women officers too.

Netiva Ben Yehuda was immediately withdrawn from the front line and sent to Upper Galilee.

> We started this school for Army recruits on the Lebanon border but they forgot to tell the Arabs we were there for peaceful purposes (sic). They came across the border to help the Palestinians and started attacks on us. There was no choice, then, and I had to fight, woman or not. I fought for a long time and it was not good – the Arabs couldn't stand it and the Jews couldn't stand it.
>
> This is not an enemy to put women opposite because all it does is raise the enemy's motivation. One doesn't look for ways to strengthen the enemy – one does the opposite.

She believes women make better fighters than men because they are more rational, but found the Jewish men couldn't accept women's part in armed struggle either, especially as officers.

> Men joined the Palmach who had not been trained in the youth movement since childhood for equality and feminism; they came, not from the kibbutz but from the coffee houses of Tel Aviv. They became my subordinates and they couldn't bear that . . . a man who goes home to Tel Aviv, to his family would say 'My commander is Netiva'. He couldn't stand it . . . it was bad for morale.

Since 1948 the careful selection of young Jewish men and women for specialist jobs in the defence force has been refined and developed: 'Every year since then they've taken the top of the milk . . . every year they take the best for Intelligence, the Air Force, frog-men. They follow those kids from childhood.'

Tamar Livney, about to go into the Army at 19, bore her out:

> I'm going in November, but I've already been given a job. I'll be in Intelligence.
> They wanted me because of both languages – the Hebrew and the English that I have. I've been interviewed many times and it's taken many tests. In the end they're not taking me for my languages, rather because of my ambition to do something for the country. They've asked me to do different things: I can't exactly tell you what! My ambition to help is very big, and I think that's what getting me far in the service.

Tamar's commitment is not felt by all the young women of Israel who are eligible for the Army, as Arab women are not. Those who are religious do not have to serve the mandatory two years; and – as Dalia Elkana shows – some of those who do serve find the task inhuman and degrading. Dalia first spoke of the work she had to do at the Allenby Bridge across the Jordan to *Hotam*, the weekend supplement of the Israeli paper *al-Ha'mishmar*.

You are Fatmah, one of the women who enter my cubicle. I order you to undress, but first I ask for your name and check your ID. You pass me the documents, sometimes with embarrassment and at other times showing hate or fear . . . this is what happens on the bridges over the Jordan, where we arrived in an Egged bus[2] driven by a fat woman whose hair is dyed a shrill blonde.

Now our hands lie in our lap or light endless cigarettes; tomorrow they will search the clothes of Arab women, look for all kinds of contrabrand at the entrance to Greater Israel, and for the potential components of a bomb. . . . We were a group of young women aged around 22. Some had come from the University, from the humanities department. Others had been studying art history or philosophy or literature. Some came from the College of Nursing.

We passed the refugee camp at Jericho, all crumbling and wretched, on our way to the base, where we changed into uniform and were given instruction in how to be alert: to stop the smuggling in of explosives, to protect the security of the State, while retaining one's human face. After all, the Arabs returning from Amman to Israel are human beings. We were posted to the Allenby Bridge, where there are two checkpoints – one for Arabs and one for tourists.

So I am now doing body searches. You, Fatmah, are one of the women who descend from the bus that has just arrived from Amman. You are returning from a visit to your relatives, or perhaps your husband, or from the burial of an uncle or aunt. You may arrive with four or five kids or by yourself, you can be a student from Bir Zeit University, or someone who studied in the United States or Britain. You may speak English, you are rich or poor, sometimes sick or blind and sometimes strong as an ox. Sometimes you smell of the land, you have strong, hard hands, and sometimes you smell of expensive perfume. In different circumstances, we might be sitting on the same bench at University.

2 Egged is the national bus company of Israel.

From the bus, you pass into the hands of the woman reservist who only yesterday attended classes. Today she is a soldier and does your body search. She looks for something sharp with which you might suddenly stab us, for bombs, explosives, knives, sharp scissors. Her hands check your head scarf, in case you have hidden something there, then the chest; you raise your arms and she goes down to the waist. Nothing – you are sent to sit with the others under a corrugated iron roof. You wait with the other men, women, children ... closed circuit television monitors your moves.

The porters, dressed in blue like kibbutzniks, are Arabs who have arrived from Jericho. They have already been searched. They unload your luggage, all the parcels, cases, carpets and blankets, for which you get a ticket. With your hand luggage you move on to another set of benches, waiting before a blue door with twenty, thirty other women, until a woman soldier tells you to come in. She cheks with a metal detector for anything sharp, again. She throws away all the food on the spot, although you are hungry. Anything suspect is confiscated; sanitary pads and nappies are forbidden. Then out again: you have now entered the Land of Israel and there is a smell of disinfectant and new rows of benches.

Here you wait until you are called by a soldier using a louspeaker. She returns your documents once everything has been filed and found in order. We know who enters and who leaves, who returns and from where. We know everybody, and you must stand in a queue until your name is called, then it's on to yet another waiting room, where a sign says We Have To Perform Body Searches for Security Reasons. Sometimes up to a hundred women wait there for hours.

You hand in your money at a long desk. It is counted and put in a plastic bag and the amount listed on your form, so that you cannot claim it has been stolen. Then you have to part with your shoes, which you throw into a huge plastic container ...

You wonder how you'll ever find them again among so

many others. The porter takes the container to be X-rayed, together with the parcels, the blankets, everything. Finally, you reach the head of the queue, and I tell you in Arabic to enter the search cubicle. As you get up, our eyes meet, and I can tell you know what happens now. You must be embarrassed, or angry, or full of hatred, but I'm not allowed to show any feelings. I must be in control. I don't speak Arabic; most of the girls working here don't speak your language. We have been taught a few words and given a phrase book.

I know how to ask your name, demand your documents, check your number. Do you speak Hebrew or English, no? That's bad. 'Undress, take everything off, everything' I tell you. I search your hand luggage, confiscate the lipstick, the deodorant, the scent in a non-transparent bottle, your make-up, any pens. Also forbidden are sanitary pads, nappies, opaque key rings, face creams and handkerchiefs. In my stumbling Arabic, I say to you: 'That is forbidden, this is confiscated', and today you submit, you say 'Okay, take it all'.

Then I act as the censor, while you take off yet another layer of clothes and shouts and crying can be heard from other cubicles. We both want to get it over. I take away all your letters, every scrap of paper, even if it contains only one word: every address will go into a plastic bag for examination. I hope it does not contain the address of a terrorist gang, I hope you are not a terrorist . . . I am sending all your family pictures to censorship.

Now you are naked, except for your underpants, and I pass the metal detector over your body. It hums quietly and checks you have not hidden some scrap of paper, drugs, money . . . I check between your toes and inside your underpants, but there is nothing, you are clear. I also check your clothes with the detector and tear open any seam that looks suspect. I look into every pocket. Then you may dress again; I fill in your forms, list everything I have confiscated . . . I tell you to sign here, and although you sometimes don't know how to write, you do as you're told.

At the next waiting room the porter brings the shoes, spilling them onto the large, high table. You have to look for them – everyone is pushing and searching. With your shoes and your number you leave that hall, but your journey into the Land of Israel is not over yet: now your suitcases are checked and they confiscate any electrical equipment that seems suspect.

Sometimes I ask whether you feel humiliated by all this. You may not reply because you think I'm interrogating you, but occasionally you say Yes. There is tension between us. I don't really succeed in explaining that I regret what I have to do. You answer, half ironically, that it is my duty – I feel ashamed. I have nothing to say. Sometimes we, the soldier girls, are afraid of you or hate you, and sometimes we are apologetic and try to break the tension by smiling. How can I confiscate all your makeup? I let it slip through, you smile, we understand one another . . . but sometimes it makes trouble: they seize a letter and a gold chain and send you back for another body search with someone else. I am called in and reprimanded. You cheated me and I am cross, although I understand.

They let you go, but the women who come after you are searched again and again, and now I am no longer soft. I watch as the mothers come in with their crying children. They have to undress them in my cubicle, and also change them there, although that is forbidden. I search all the babies, and their nappies, including the dirty ones. I also check the used sanitary pads; even if you have your periods I still search you.

Sometimes you are sick, or pretend to be, and you ask me to help you undress. If you look really unwell, I will help you dress again and bring you water, and you might kiss my hand, or even my feet until I tell you to stop it. Today I undressed one woman who had a black rag in her bra. 'Take it out,' I ordered, and she did, revealing a hole instead of a breast. We looked at one another and she was smiling. I was in shock. 'Get dressed,' I said, helping to bandage again the scars and stitches from the operation.

In my first week I was embarrassed, ashamed and disgusted. I used to speak in a quiet voice. I tried to be kind, but slowly I lost my humanity. I became impatient, began to feel they were all trying to cheat me. After they had caught you, Fatmah, with the letter and the gold chain, I wondered whether you also had explosives although I had searched you so carefully. I think I became paranoid; had I stayed another week, the tension would have exploded.

Gradually that job takes you over. You have difficulty remembering that these are women like yourself. But there are people who actually enjoy doing it, especially among those who search the men. We, the girls, tried to retain some of our sanity, to observe certain limits wherever possible, but I cannot say that we succeeded.

Dalia Elkana, like so many other Israeli men and women, is trapped. This is one result of forty years of Statehood and a hundred years on from the aspiration to resettle in Palestine, a result that reverberates with symbolism. Dalia herself may only have to take this unpleasant duty once or twice during her Army service but thousands of her compatriots face similar tasks every day. Israelis angrily cite Palestinian terrorism if one asks questions about Army techniques and military control, but no one seems to question why that terrorism – surely a form of war – takes place inside and outside Israel so continuously. Have there not been real opportunities to negotiate peace? After 1967, for example, whe the IDF's great success placed the government in a strong position to be magnaminous? It has become difficult to believe that the serious pursuit of peace negotiations, which would provide the Palestinians with the possibility of an independent and autonomous life not ground between Israel, Jordan and the other Arab powers, has a place on the government's agenda. For Dalia, and those she has to search, the result is acute misery – a situation for the women in the Army quite as traumatic as border patrols and fighting for men. The consequences of terror and military domination mean that all have to breathe a daily air suffused with fear, mistrust and anger.

Colonel Amira Dotan, as the former commander of the Women's Army, Chen, was the person in charge of Tamar Livney and Dalia Elkana. She does not question defence policies; commitment for her is an unquestioned premise upon which women's own growth can take place within the Army framework:

Here in Israel we know, from the moment we can understand, that at the age of 18 or 19 we are going to be soldiers. Our everyday life shows that to be a soldier is not to be theoretical, or some chocolate soldier. It is really to take on active duty and to do things – last year it could be Lebanon, before then it was Sinai or Ramat Ha Golan or whatever. It is doing something for your country, really acting.

Besides, as I see it, we women in Israel live in two different worlds of values. There are the Jewish values, the tradition that the place of the woman is within her family and home. She is very much honoured; and she has to be a mother and a wife to her husband. And as well as this world there is the twentieth century or twenty-first century world of values, in which a woman has to be independent to fulfil herself.

As I feel and see it – and I'm a Sabra – it's a clash; all of us, but especially those women who work outside the home, feel this struggle. When we look at the IDF it's male orientated, like armed forces all over the world. Men are there to take the decisions, to make policy: we women are there to do other things. And the main work is to fight. It's only in the past few years that we realised we want to be in on the decision-making, but not on the fighting. Till then we were happy to be very lively, just very feminine women.

Now I must re-educate the young, especially the officers, because I feel that through them the new generation of new leaders will grow. They'll do more than we've done, but they'll still remain women: they'll realise their full potential. But to achieve that you have to put more in. For instance, men serve three years in the Army and women two – but in that time they cannot handle the new technology or the computers.

So they come at 18, very wonderful and often clever, but with no education in this new world . . . from the beginning there are two minuses: no skill in technology and only a two year stay. I beg them to take preliminary courses at school, but we really have to change attitudes – not only theirs but their mothers'. When we started the electronics course only 22 girls did it; now it's already more than 300.

I don't think women should drop bombs or become pilots, though. That goes back to the traditions of Judaism and also, because we are stationed here in Israel, it is allied to the Muslim tradition. We can fight, we could be pilots – it's not a matter of ability but one of values that stops us. Besides, women spend only four years in the Reserve after their training and men go on till they're 50 or 55. No, we're helping with general skills more than the fighting ones. We are taught how to use a gun, but that's for emergencies. And learning things like computer training is wonderful because you can gain a lot of money.

We did not intend to call the women's army Chen, which means 'grace'. Chen really stands for Chet Nune, women's corps, but the name pleased a lot of women at first. They thought that, as women in uniform, it was their role to be only charming. I think we are much more than that – we have at last started with equal opportunities and equal rights. That happened in 1984, after I became commander. But I don't think we shall see the Chief of Staff a woman; it needs to be somebody who really did some fighting.

I think our women officers are good and wonderful and they can do a lot of jobs. I am pushing them to believe that they do have the power and the strength to take on new responsibility – and I also push the men to believe this. Now, after three years of equal chances, the male officers say the women have real potential, even if they lack the experience of fighting on the battlefield.

This does not mean, as the commander of Chen, that I have to ask any man for permission to do anything when it comes to my women soldiers. I am the highest professional in this field. So when it comes to how they live, and what will be the contents of a course – whatever is concerned with women who are serving in the IDF – everybody has to ask me and not the other way around. Our Chief of Staff really does that: he asks me. From the beginning, when I started this work, he has cooperated wonderfully. People ask me how, when I am so feminine and not aggressive, how come that they listen? I think my power is that I believe in what I am doing, and I believe in the power of women.

My own life is not easy. I got this position when I was 35, a young woman I think. Even for a male officer it would be very nice to get to such a place at this age. My parents were very proud of me, but in the same sentence they said 'But oh, what will you do with your children? They will lack your presence.' We are always in the same conflict. What is our task? When you are 25 you have your first child and there is an expectation that you will be a mother and you will raise children. So from 25 to 32 you are dedicated to your home, your children, your husband, everything. But this is also the time when you have to develop your other skills, so there is an active conflict. A few women succeed in surviving both . . . you can do it, but the price is high.

Fathers today spend a lot of time in the kitchen, and with the children – more time than they used to, or their fathers did, but even so our guilt feelings as women and as wives follow us. I leave the home to do my own thing, and he'll be with the children, but I still worry.

I'm a mother, a career woman and a psychologist. So I'm not here in this position in the IDF because of lack of money or because I have no alternatives. I am proud of what I do and I hold a lot of power. I am not going to ask anyone what to do with Chen, which is really a school for life, our lives here in Israel. Chen teaches young women to live independently: you have to think what you want to do, you have to choose between alternatives – it makes you a grown-up person.

The most important thing about Chen is not the work – the communications, the aides, the medical corps: it is that it is compulsory. You have to cope with life, and with war . . . and you grow up.

Dana Arieli had recently finished her Army service when we met; like Colonel Dotan, she felt the experience was beneficial for young Jewish women. Her idealism and sense of service had been untarnished by her support for the Peace Now movement in its campaign against the war in Lebanon.

Before I went into the Army I graduated at one of the best high schools in Israel. I was very spoilt: as an only child I got everything I wanted. The first day in the Army showed me that if someone tells me to wake up at five o'clock in the morning I must do it, whether I want to or not. I discovered that other people exist as well, and that I have to get along with them and live with them pleasantly . . .

I started my service at 18 in Sarafan, close to Tel Aviv. I was sent to Sinai after three weeks: at that time we were to give back Yamit to the Egyptians, according to the peace treaty. It was a tough job, trying to say to my own people – people very different from me, extreme in their opinions, but still Israelis – that they had to leave their homes. They were hard to deal with. We stayed there a month – the first two weeks without even being able to take a shower! Everything was happening very quickly, but I did realise that I wasn't just doing a job for the Army in Yamit – the politics of it did matter. I began to form opinions; it was very hard.

I went back to Sarafan and was put on a commander's course and then I began running three-week induction courses for other girls, 60–70 at a time. They were all brand new in the Army, exactly as I'd been just a few months earlier: being a commander in Chen doesn't mean leading a group to fight, because we're not fighting. The right way to do it is to be human. You have to be a good example and a good listener. I came to the conclusion that serving in the Army was not such a bad thing to do.

By the way, women commanders can command men as well as women. I wasn't afraid of commanding guys, but their base was in Ramallah, on the West Bank, and my mother was against me travelling over the Green line that we crossed when we made the new military zone in 1967. So I was negative about that.

After the commander training and the induction courses I went on an officer's course. Then I started some new and interesting work: there were girls in the Army who did not have the proper educational level. When they came in, they had to have three months induction, not three weeks – I began to work with them. When they came out, they would be better citizens . . .

Part of my Army life meant that I had to walk 25–30 miles a week with a heavy gun and high boots. My hair was tucked under a cap and I was carrying 15 kilos. But it was easy to come back to my senses and my personality – to come back to being a woman. I think that what the Army did for me was not to brutalise me, but to knock the naïvete out of me. We had to visit hospitals, with all the wounded from the Lebanon war – sometimes we packed parcels for the soldiers in the north, from midnight until nine in the morning.

It changed your whole perspective, changed your point of view: it makes you an adult long before you would be in any other society . . . Israelis of 22, as I am now, are far more mature than the people I met on my travels. And as a commander I had to be tough; you're an example and you have to be the first in everything . . . you must give orders. The Army made me a feminist, because I felt I could do everything I want – it helped me to deal with and cope with everything I want to do now. I believe I'm equal now with others.

When Dana finished her Army service she spent seven months travelling in Europe: she realised then that living in Israel made a demand for close political commitment. She decided to become a political science student: 'That kept me close to daily events, as well as their political meaning. I realised, too, how intense Israelis are in their daily involvement and concern; I had found no other country where people listen to the news on the radio every hour as we do: most Israelis do that.' I wondered whether that had as much to do with the

daily fear of attack on individuals or groups, which involves the
Army in arduous guard duty and a continual Alert.

I decided I belonged on the left and as the largest party, the
Ma'arach (the Labour grouping), did not reflect my own
opinions persuasively enough I began to look at everything
else. It came very naturally, since I had many friends there, to
join Shalom Akshav (Peace Now).

I became familiar with their ideas in a more detailed way,
although the things had already been in my mind since the
Lebanon war started in 1982 – that was when I started
thinking that maybe things were going wrong. For me, like
the other citizens of Israel, the aims of the Lebanon war – at
the beginning – were quite clear; and I agreed with them.

That aim, to give security to the people who live in the
north, seemed right to me: why should a girl who lives in
Kiryat Shmona, in the north, have to sit in a shelter while I,
in Jerusalem, had a free life? And the aim of getting the
Palestinians 40 kilometres away from our border seemed
quite logical to me at the beginning. As far as the things that
were negative – killing Lebanese, that was terrible. It wasn't
an aim that had been loudly put forward, or organised, but
since the citizens of Lebanon and the PLO were all together,
living together, there were of course a lot of people killed. I
don't agree with the Palestinians, because I don't agree with
terrorism at all . . . but after a period the aims of the war
were no longer clear, and I didn't feel safe with the people
who were running it, and losing it.

The people representing me – the Prime Minister, the
Defence Minister Ariel Sharon – they were making a mess.

I'm very concerned about democracy in Israel. Look what
happened when the Arab terrorists were released after the
Lebanon war – three Jewish soldiers for more than a
thousand Arabs: it was a heavy price to pay for the precious
lives of our soldiers. But it's not something to argue
about – it's one of our agreements, that an Israeli life is
precious, and I agree with that. The trouble started after the
release when the extreme right said that if the Arab terrorists

were released, the Jewish ones – the people who had thrown bombs in Bethlehem and Hebron – should also come out. There's no way a democracy can release those who haven't been judged, and a murderer is a murderer, it's the same whether Arab or Jew..

It was a turning point for me. We had the fear that the war in Lebanon would destroy our democracy and our proper system of judicial law. So when we demonstrated in Shalom Akhshav, it was not only for an end to that war, but also to make sure that the Jews, like the Arabs, had a proper trial for terrorist acts – no matter what happened to them after the judgment. We fear very much that our democracy, the only democracy in the Middle East, is under a major threat from the right in this country.

It isn't true to say that only Arabs use terrorism . . . in fact before the establishment of the State in 1948 Jews were using it – look at the killing of Count Bernadotte by the Stern Gang, the murder of Arlosoroff,[3] the Zionists killing De Haan[4] when he tried to make peace with Abdullah. Who invented terrorism? There have always been extreme parties in Israel, with major disagreements about what they wanted for the country, but some of those actions early in our history had a big effect on the future State.

Some of the right-wing groups try to ignore the 600,000 Arabs who live in Israel, or they want to get rid of them. There is no way you can say this population does not exist . . . the cars of Arabs have a different colour number plate from the car I have – it shocks me every time I see it. Their colour is blue and mine is yellow. It reminds me of the

3 *Arlosoroff.* Chaim Arlosoroff was the director of the political department of the Jewish Agency. He was regarded as conciliatory in his efforts to improve Arab–Israeli understanding and was mysteriously assassinated in 1935.

4 *De Haan*   Jacob De Haan (1881–1924) was a Dutch poet and journalist who went to live an Orthodox Jewish life in Jerusalem. He became a spokesperson for the Jewish Ashkenazi Council but was assassinated for 'intriguing with Arabs'. It was regarded as the first political assassination carried out by Jews.

yellow stars that Jews had to wear under the Nazis, so that everyone knew who they were.

I'm friendly with a young Arab student at the University who has not, of course, been in the Army.[5] He is finishing his chemistry degree and doing well. But the lecturers in his department at the Hebrew University are hostile to him. They say to him 'Don't do an Arab job', which is a racist expression that's used here in talking about second rate work. That is not the only thing Rassid has to deal with: although he will get a good grade, he does not think he will get a job because the lecturers have already said that they will not give him a reference, just because he is an Arab.

Yesterday we were all swimming in the pool together when the news came on: there was an item about a guy being killed in a motor car accident. At the end the announcer said he was an Arab and one of the Jewish girls said 'Well, that doesn't matter, then.' Rassid just stood there . . .

I visited Ulpan Akiva on a sunny Monday morning as a three week course in Hebrew and another in Arabic was about to begin. The Ulpan is housed in a simple beachside motel south of Netania and more than a hundred people – women and men, old, young, Israeli and foreign – had gathered for intensive study. They had been seconded by the Army, the Department of Justice, Universities. The young women in khaki uniform among them had been through a series of rigorous tests before being chosen for the Arab course. Why had they come?

I think it's important to learn Arabic because we live here with them and we must know their language. We live together, but they are our enemies . . . if we know the language we will understand them better.

---

5 *Arabs/Army*   Arab men who live in Israel are not conscripted into the Israeli Defence Force, although some Bedouin and Druze do join up on a voluntary basis. As Army service affects the level of benefits received by the family as a whole, welfare for Arabs within Israel is usually considerably less than that received by Jewish Israelis.

I hope they will not be our enemies for ever . . . I would like to see peace, like everyone, but I don't see any solution right now.

The friend sitting next to her at the coffee table agreed:

I'm the same. I like the language and now, when I think of it, I think it's important to learn it. We need it in daily life, when we speak to Arabs – and it will be the way they speak with us, although they all learn Hebrew. And also for the Army it's important – for the defence of the country.

Someone else said:

They know a lot about the Jews, about our way of life, our culture. We must learn about them.

There were others there from the Army as well – mostly men working in the military administration of the West Bank or Gaza – and a lawyer from the Department of Justice. All felt that learning Arabic would help them in their tasks; they were pragmatic in their approach and did not see a future of closer relations with the Arabs they saw every day.

Irene Hirschmann of Haifa feels it is war rather than Army service and conscription (Israel is one of only four countries in the world where women are conscripted) that has fundamentally affected women's lives:

The fact that Israel has been in a state of war for so many years, and that the Army is based on the whole people of Israel makes our lives what they are, because even when a man is 40 or 50 and he has a family he still joins the war. It's not only a regular standing army. So everybody expects the women to stick to their conservative role as the glue of the family . . . it has happened to many women that the father, the husband and the son went to the war: everyone expected the woman to stay at home and to look after the family affairs, to be a good mother, to be a good daughter, a good sister to the soldiers who are at war. That is much more important than her job in the Army.

There is enormous patriotism and it affects us. I believe that women who consider themselves feminists could be seen as betraying the existence of Israel, if at a time of war they let themselves worry about their own problems. The rights of women are less important then the State of Israel.

I think it's a false dichotomy, myself. You can worry about this and that at the same time and I don't think looking after the problem of women's rights has anything to do with it. You can be a very good mother, and a very good daughter, a wife, and still worry about your rights. I think it's a tragedy, the way things are here . . . and it's not a political trick, because if it had been you could say that this party, or that party, would allow more women's rights than the other one, but it hasn't been like that at all.

No – it comes from the fact that men will never give up power without a struggle. Here they have everything on their side: law, custom, the Talmud. Also we women are not united enough – those women who talk about self-fulfilment and women's rights have not been able to gain the sympathy or the interest of others. Often they get hostility from them instead! You must also remember that a lot of Israeli women came from countries where they had no conception of such things – if the husband beats that woman, she doesn't think about her rights, she only thinks she has a problem.

You just can't say that all the women can talk the same language: it's a multi-layered, multi-cultural, pluralistic society.

I left Irene as her daughter, 18-year-old Sharon, arrived on weekend leave after her first three months in the Army. Poised and self-confident, she saw her service as a glamorous time; she hoped to do well enough in her coming examinations to be chosen for an officer's training course. But many women – as many as 40 per cent – don't go into the Army at all, in spite of conscription. They plead a devout adherence to the Jewish faith as the reason they cannot serve, and do social or community work instead. (Far fewer men are able to avoid service

1 Now a dynamic political leader, Geula Cohen supported terrorist methods in the struggle against the British Mandate. Today she is a tireless fighter for a 'Greater Israel' that would include all the West Bank.

2 Shoshana Mageni has eight children but wants to have at least four more. Mass Jewish population growth is vital if Jews are to outstrip the Arabs whom she regards as inferior and potentially dangerous.

3 Jerusalem born and bred, Zahera Kamal has to report to the police twice daily although she has never been charged with a crime.

4 Pnina Herzog is the sister-in-law of the President of Israel. She has a strong social conscience and works for the World Health Organisation.

5 In the Ultra-Orthodox Mea'h She'arim area of Jerusalem, men reign so supreme that women have to pray outside the synagogue.

6 Hiam Abbass has broken away from life in an Arab village in Galilee to become an actress. It took two years for her parents to become reconciled to the idea of her marriage to an Englishman, even though he became a Muslim.

7 Israeli born, Sima Waxman meets prejudice from fellow Jews who regard her as a Moroccan because her parents emigrated from there.

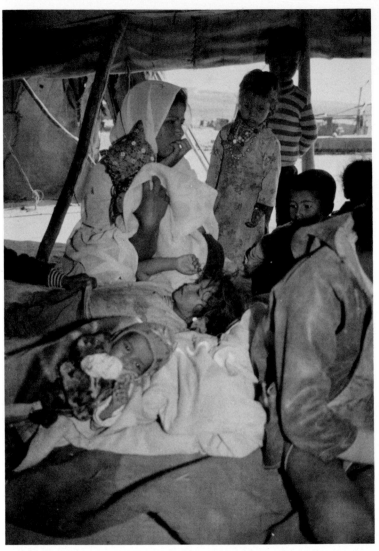

8a Bedouin women near Beersheva, adapting to a fresh life that is no longer nomadic.

8b Gradually, the black-winged traditional tents are giving way to breeze-block and cement.

8c Infant mortality rates are high among the Bedouin of the Negev and medical services infrequent.

altogether; instead, they join a religious corps that does not serve in the front line.) No Arab women are conscripted but a few Druze have joined as volunteers.

You cannot spend a single day in Israel without being throbbingly aware of the military presence: everywhere, most of the time. People are being guarded, or guarded against; buildings are on the defensive. Roadblocks are frequent and discriminate between the owners of different coloured number plates. Body searches are a norm. It doesn't stop the conflict at home or abroad, and it has a dulling and a brutalising effect on doers as well as those done to. I think some of the most unhappy faces I've ever seen are among the young men and women in uniform whom I saw on patrol, searching cars, doing guard duty. Sharon's idea of a glamorous life was a long way off . . . theirs was a permanent tension, a continual watchfulness. I found it difficult to believe they are any more free than the Palestinians they watch struggle for their rights.

The brutalisation comes out in other ways, too. Carmit Gie, an Israeli television news reader:

> Part of the reason men are so macho here is their Army experience. When I was doing my military service in an office, men would come in — lawyers, doctors — people who had been drinking from porcelain cups the day before — and turn into beasts: swearing, making passes and behaving in ways they would never dream of at home.

CHAPTER 3

JERUSALEM
THE GOLDEN

I visited Jerusalem for the first time with Miriam Halevi, who had lived there for many years before the Six Day war in 1967 brought it fully under Israeli control. As a socialist she believes in equal sharing, but as a Zionist she is certain that Israel needs the whole city, and not just parts of it, to maintain itself there in safety. Although she is not a devout person, she went to the West Wall – the Wailing Wall – after the victory in 1967: 'I had the feeling that I had to say this prayer, thanking God for having seen that day when Jerusalem was no longer cut in half and we could feel safe.' It was not long before she regretted her action, because the acquisition of East Jerusalem had also meant 'taking the rest of the West Bank. That has been a disaster for us – just us; I'm not even speaking about how it affects the Arabs. You cannot be a democratic nation and rule a million people who do not want to be ruled by you. It has turned all of us, men and women, into the army of occupation, a nation of occupation . . . what has it done to our own freedoms and our civilised behaviour?'

Unlike the rest of the West Bank, East Jerusalem has been incorporated formally into Israel and is no longer occupied territory. But this magnificent city clearly still has two halves, The West, with tall buildings in the local limestone and golden-rose alabaster shading wider streets, or the narrow older ones of the religious quarter, is full of zest and exhilarating life. The East, although full of tourists who cram the holy places and the Old City, has many empty spaces, rubble-laden fields and a no-man's land look in spite of some easing of building restrictions in 1981. Jews live in the West, Arabs in the East – not quite, because immediately beyond the inner city area there are thick concrete rinds: the new suburbs and apartments, each with their own bomb shelter, that house the young Jewish families who will help maintain Jerusalem as a Jewish city 'for ever' whatever the international community may say.

The two parts barely speak to each other. There are exceptions – and not only those linked with the common predilection for fragrant Arab food – but there is an over-whelming sense that Jews do not see Arabs or Arabs meet Jews, visit them or share their lives except in the most formal of necessary circumlocutions. People stare at each other with blind eyes. I asked a Jewish woman who is married to an Arab if we could tape an interview: she was afraid of the possible consequences; he might be physically attacked and she was already experiencing discrimination.

Some small breaks in that rigid isolationism are now attacked by the Right. Early in 1986 one of Israel's Chief Rabbis, Mordechai Eliyahu, issued the ruling 'It is forbidden to sell apartments in the land of Israel to Gentiles' in response to questions about the sale and letting of flats to Arabs in Neveh Yacov, one of the new suburbs on the West Bank. The Chief Rabbi then amplified his first statement – there was to be no letting to Muslims either; Christians were idolators and only three flats per suburb could be let to them. On the day of the second ruling the home of one of the few Arab families in Neveh Yavoc, the Jaabars, was set alight and one of their eleven children, 4-year-old Swaafi, went to hospital overcome by the smoke.

The Jewish family who lived next door to the Jaabars found their home on fire next; they were friendly with their Arab neighbours. In a letter signed 'Kach' they were warned that their children would be killed, their home razed to the ground if they continued the friendship.

At the time of the fire-bombs, Shulamit Berger wrote to the newspaper *Ha'aretz* about a friend:

An honest man who holds a responsible job, is a loyal friend and spends his spare time doing voluntary public work – in short, a true representative of the beautiful Israel. Recently this man decided to sell his flat in Neveh Yacov and move to a larger one. He was approached by several interested parties, among them three Arabs. He explained to the three that he was in favour of equal rights for Arabs, but did not feel that Jews and Arabs should live together. Therefore, he said, he would not sell to them. At the end of one such conversation, the Arab he was talking to told him that he was used to being refused because of his origins, but that this was the first time someone had admitted the real reason rather than give some poor excuse. My acquaintance, who is not a rich man, sold his flat in the end for substantially less than he could have obtained from any of the potential Arab buyers.

These days, an Arab from a village near Neveh Yacov is spending the cold winter in Jerusalem's jail because he cannot afford to pay the six million (old) Shekel fine imposed on him for building his home without a permit. It is, in fact, almost impossible to obtain building permits from the municipality.

True, the law is the same for both Jewish and Arab citizens, and they must observe it. However, what is a man supposed to do when people do not want to sell to him here, and he is not allowed to build there?

In another part of East Jerusalem, Zahera Kamal is the first to get up every morning. She dresses and eats in quiet and solitude and then takes a long walk to the nearest police detention centre in West Jerusalem, Mosqobia. She has had to report there twice a day for the past six years under the rules of her town arrest order; she has been incarcerated, and an Amnesty International prisoner of the month even though she was never charged with any crime. Zahera was born in Jerusalem; she is as much a citizen as Shulamit Berger or Miriam Halevi, but her life has been circumscribed in innumerable ways ever since she came back from Cairo University to teach physics at a teacher training college on the West Bank.

I was prevented from teaching at the beginning. In 1978 I was interrogated, and again in 1979 – then I was on administrative detention for six months. I appealed to a higher court and was released the day before my appeal was to be heard. Then I was town arrested and prevented from going to work for forty-five days. I went to the college headquarters, which are near my home, and arranged to work in the office there, teaching my students by sending them the material and getting it back every day so that I didn't lose my job. Then I had permission to go to work one day a week, and at least I was able to discuss their difficulties with the students. Now, at last, I can teach every day, but I have to sign at the police station at seven thirty on my way to school and again on my return.

Zahera Kamal is active against the occupation and is chairwoman of the Women's Work Committee which does political and educational work among Arab women on the West Bank. She resents the continual supervision to which she is subjected but it does not prevent her from carrying on the work: 'We want to change the life of women here. That means literacy classes, social work – and much more than that: we're aiming at the full liberation of women as a part of the restoration of our national rights.'
Zahera is not married:

I live with my family: my mother and brothers and sisters. We're a big family – six girls and two boys. I think we may be unique because we believe that women must be equal with men: all of us believe it. My brothers help in all the work at home, and we respect each other. They share everything – the cooking, the cleaning. My mother was perhaps a little old-fashioned; she didn't really want her daughters to go out to work, but she didn't try to stop us. It's not only among Palestinian families that men find its not their work to cook and clean! You don't usually find it in Western families, and even less among Palestinians.

The traditional picture of a Muslim family is very different from the way roles and rituals are fashioned in the Kamal family. Mostly, women are subservient and domesticity takes the place of education. Even to seek work outside the home is seen as the stigma of poverty by many of those whose husbands and fathers have a comfortable income.

Zahera's committee concentrates on literacy classes because most of the older women on the West Bank cannot read or write. Girls go to school, but in rural parts of Israel and the occupied territories most drop out at the end of primary school. Arab children are educated separately from Jewish boys and girls, a custom supported by most members of both groups. There are Arab advisers in the Ministry of Education but the Prime Minister's own adviser on Arab affairs is Jewish – hardly the way forward to a shining understanding. And there are twanging strings between Education, which is officially committed to schemes to try and improve understanding between the two groups – and even provides some notional funds in that direction for the Van Leer Foundation's Learning to Live Together scheme – and Religious Affairs, which works to prevent any meetings between Arab and Jewish pupils, worried that togetherness could breed trouble, even to the point of the intermarriage which is against Jewish religious law.

Jewish schools, in comparison with their Arab neighbours both within Israel and in Gaza and the West Bank, have ten times more funding. Teachers' pay is the only point of parity between the two; books, equipment, buildings, sport – those are mostly provided for by the local authority, and the government statistics show the comparative wealth of the Jewish authorities. In addition, Jewish schools attract all sorts of other subventions, from the religious to the charitable. I visited schools where there were no books at all and others with excellent libraries: the difference was regularly one of religion rather than class.

It has not always been like that. The Jerusalem author Netiva Ben Yehuda remembers better times. So does Mary Khass, who now lives in Gaza:

I went to the English high school in Haifa – that was shared between Jews and Palestinians, both Muslim and Christian. There was a very good atmosphere until 1946, when demonstrations started . . . either Jewish or Palestinian students. I had many friends there, of all kinds. After 1948, and in spite of the war, it was impossible to stop seeing my friends – we used to sneak through the barbed wire and borders to see each other and be with each other. While the war was on I used to visit a Jewish friend – I remember one time some boys heard us speaking English, because I didn't speak Hebrew. They said, 'You should learn Hebrew'. I was very stupid, and I said, 'No, why should I; I'm an Arab' – you can imagine how frightened my friends were for my safety.

But even before the war there had been resentment when the Arab community had been told to move into two areas in Haifa.

It was quite humiliating, and difficult for us to accept. Suddenly, we could not live in any part of Haifa, as we had . . . it was the creation of a ghetto! Suddenly, we could only live in certain streets, nowhere else.

Before 1948, Netiva Ben Yehuda says 'You can't imagine, we learned in schools together, in the Universities together, we used to dance together in the cabaret . . . Jews and Arabs all mixed . . . on the trains, on the buses: it's unimaginable today.' She feels the present rocklike polarity, the growing hatred, to be the result of two nationalisms:

Yes, like us they are nationalistic and are entitled to somewhere to live, a country and a motherland . . . it's our story all over again. The two movements started together but we managed better than they. It has also led to the terrible law of the Jew, the Law of Return[1]: when you come here you are immediately, on the spot, a citizen. You know this law? It is a racial law. All Zionism is racial when you come to think of it; at the beginning when this race didn't have enough

1 The Law of Return: on arrival in Israel every Jew (but it applies only to Jews) has immediate rights of citizenship. Arabs who were born there also have those rights; those on the West Bank carry Jordanian passports and the 600,000 people of Gaza are stateless.

people or enough territory you could swallow it, but every day now, every year that passes it's getting worse and worse.

What has it meant to my old Arab friends from college days? Every single one of them has left the country . . . not one of them is in Israel. They can't stand it here. As Jews, if we can't stand it, still most of us stay, but they can go to Saudi, or Kuwait, or Libya, where they are thought of as an elite. A three-week plumber's course in Israel turns you into a skilled engineer as far as the others are concerned, because Israeli skill training is highly regarded. But of course a great many don't want to emigrate: and why should they have to?

Jewish children have compulsory, free education until they're 16. Then parents find the money for books; in addition, many pay extra so that their children – especially the boys – can attend a high school where the religious content of the curriculum is high. (At the end of that continuum are yeshiva schools where, from an early age, boys learn only the Torah and the Talmud: they are intended for the contemporary world, but within the confines of the rabbinate.) Schools are streamed, with psycho-educational testing at 12 and again at 15, and at that time girls who are judged non-academic are encouraged in the direction of nursing, kindergarten work or basic office skills. In fact most of the young women I met who had gone down that road were of Sephardi descent: the Ashkenazis mostly went to University when they had done their Army service.

Ora, just 15, had just taken her second psychometric test at the Gymnasia Herzelia, a highly regarded Jerusalem school, when we met at a tea party:

> I could stay in my present school and not transfer to a special High School, but I don't want to. What happens is that they keep the kids they want – he or she can stay without any exam, no matter what the school work is like or how good they are. And if they don't want a particular girl to stay, she won't stay. It's not based on how good they are in school, but mainly on background. If they don't want them – like most of the kids that come from Morocco – they don't let

them stay in school, unless they're real bright.

Most of them, they just tell them, 'You don't fit into our school, and we don't want you here.' And then they go to a different school of their own background. They wanted me to stay. I'm Ashkenazi, not Sephardi. I'm not from Morocco or Yemen or Algeria. My school work was very low, and there were many Moroccan kids whose school work was higher than me, but they didn't let them to stay: they said, you'll not fit in; we want you to go.

Unless you're very, very bright, you can't stay if you're a Moroccan Jew.

I didn't want to stay in that sort of school, after they had said to us it was the Number One school for mixtures between different backgrounds and religions. 'We're the best school for that,' they said. Then, after two years of being together, they do their best just to separate us all again. At the beginning, they said, 'Everybody stays'. If they can't stick to that, at least they should do it on the basis of tests. It's such bad discrimination – and that's just among Jews!

I'd like to see all people treated the same. I don't think the Moroccans realised what was being done to them. Besides, what people do to them, they do to the Arabs, I think. Because they say to me: 'Arabs, they won't succeed at anything.' Or somebody who comes from Eastern Europe: 'Oh, they won't succeed at anything.'

I want to meet Arabs, I want to see their way of living, to try and get them to be equal with us. In the book, they're supposed to – but they're not. If you live in Israel you can see that they're not equal; they're not treated as equal. I want to see that they should be treated as equal – yes, I will meet them, but I don't think the Moroccans will. They call them cockroaches and say, 'We don't want to meet them. They have countries they should go back to. They're not part of us.'

Ora chose to go to another of Jerusalem's twenty Jewish high schools, where she finds the atmosphere more liberal, but she has still not had the opportunity of meeting any Arab high school students of the same age. That's not surprising, perhaps, in the light of the concern of the department of Religious Affairs. And also not surprising when you meet the profound depression and anger that greets guerilla attacks inside and outside the country. In one year alone, 1985, there were ten attacks abroad and dozens of smaller ones within Israel. Not all those in Rome or Vienna, Athens or Beirut were to do with Israeli affairs, but the preponderance were claimed by adherents of the Palestinian cause. In eight months of the same year the Israeli government reported that nineteen people had died and more than a hundred were injured in pursuit of that cause. Israel, with a population only one seventeenth that of Britain, has three times as many tanks and the same number of combat aircraft as the Royal Air Force. War, and now armed resistance of many different kinds, has hardened many to a cold enmity and hostility that make those young people who seek movement in the opposite direction, like Ora, a diminishing minority.

Underground activity has also affected the work of Rivka Ben Aharon. She teaches in a State religious high school in Jerusalem.

I am a religious woman. I consider myself a moderate in nearly all spheres, and agonise over the current problems of our relations with our Arab neighbours within whatever borders are eventually determined. I teach a civics programme – The Framework of the State of Israel – to a matriculation class of 27 girls and 16 boys, most of them the children of manual labourers who arrived in the mass immigration of the 1950s from Asia and North Africa. My pupils were born in Israel and are the first generation of their family ever to receive formal, organised education.

Many of the girls and boys possess an acute sense of being discriminated against within the community by other Jews. Politically – due to strong home influence – they lean strongly to the right. They admire Likud and have a blind hatred for Arabs. Their work is mediocre to weak, the boys weaker than the girls. Some of the girls belong to the Tehiya youth movement. [Tehiya is the Renaissance party led by Geula Cohen.]

Rivka Ben Aharon felt that the girls and the boys had a strong hatred for all strangers, for all non-Jews and even for Jews of a different community or a different opinion. After the Sabra and Shatilla massacres and the subsequent murder of a Peace Now demonstrator,

> I felt I had to do something to diminish the hatred even a little. I felt the values which are so important to me, and on which democracy in Israel is based – and perhaps also our moral survival in this country – were being undermined. I could not sit by idly.

She found the programme called To Live Together, published by the Van Leer Foundation in Jerusalem with support from the Ministry of Education: she began to work on it with her adolescent pupils.

> As soon as I presented the subject I encountered fierce resistance. Eighty percent of the class shouted that there was no need to learn about Arabs. 'We should learn about things that relate to us.' The raucous part of the class cried out that the Arabs should be taken and killed as fast as possible. The more 'sensitive' ones proposed, instead, deportation from the country.
>
> I decided to devote the entire remaining time of that academic year – about four months – to the subject, and every student was given the floor. I felt that the explosive atmosphere had to be defused by allowing the pupils to divest themselves of the load they were carrying. In the first stage, I did very little talking. My only argument was that in order to reject something you must know what it is you are rejecting. Their counter-claim was that they knew more about the Arabs than I did, since their parents had been born and raised in Arab lands.
>
> Around the fourth lesson I began to gain their assent to go on studying the subject: 'Perhaps we don't know so much about the Arabs, but even when we know more our hatred

won't stop: that's for sure, because it's in our blood.' We started with prejudices and stereotypes. The dominant stereotype in the class about the Arab was that he was dirty, worked with garbage, was primitive and a dangerous enemy of the country. To explain the concept of a stereotype I tried analysing stereotypes about Jews. They argued that I had no right to make that kind of comparison – the two cases were completely different.

At the end of the stereotype lesson one pupil dared say that the Arab cleaning woman at her home really was a good woman, but as a group the Arabs were enemies – the reaction of the others wasn't as fierce as it would have been when we first began studying the subject. The class had the feeling it was very easy to get caught up in stereotypes (I gave examples from our own Israeli situation – all Rumanians are seen as thieves, all Moroccans as knife-wielders . . .). The girls especially got the feeling they had to study reality in all its complexity: anyone who stuck to their prejudices refused to learn because she was afraid that study would undermine her opinions.

The study on minorities in the world was also interesting. The boys' class particularly reached the conclusion that we should actually treat any stranger in our midst harshly, since this would be a way of paying back only a small part of what had been done to us as Jews! Then, on the subject of the development of the Arab village, the pupils were patronising: 'What else do they want? Look what we gave them. Would they have given that to Jews in *their* lands?' But as soon as the programme began to touch on issues such as the legal status of Arabs, or their historic attachment to the country, passions flared up again.

I was shocked: the moment they had to apply in practice what they'd learned to the democratic basis of Israel, it was as though they'd learned nothing. They argued that it didn't matter what the Declaration of Independence[2] said about the

---

2 Declaration of Independence: passed by the Jewish National Council, it became effective when the British Mandate ended in Israel in May 1948. It says, 'The State of Israel will maintain complete equality of social and political rights for all its citizens, without distinction of creed, race or sex.'

Arabs; it wasn't important, it could be amended or expunged. I had to work very hard to explain that the principle of civic equality is unassailable, that in a democracy you couldn't just choose what was convenient for the majority – and that majority might become a minority one day.

It was the section To be an Arab in Israel, which had personal accounts by Arab pupils of their experiences, which generated the main change of attitude. Some of the girls came to class in the morning and said they'd actually been unable to sleep after reading the texts. And the girls who most identified with the personal accounts were the same ones from the Tehiya youth movement who, at the start, had been among the most aggressive. For the first time I could ask 'In the wake of what we had read, did they think that both Jews and Arabs should change their attitudes and behaviour?'

The replies were incredible. I could hardly believe that the same pupils were already having doubts, that the problem with which we had to cope began to be understood. Israel is Jewish but also a society with a non-Jewish minority; there was no alternative but to go on living together, since they did not wish to go elsewhere – they feel this is their land, too. The grasping of this problem was one of the most moving stages of the whole programme.

From that point on things were a good deal calmer. Most of the pupils had undergone a significant shift, emotionally and in terms of their knowledge. All felt there was a problem here which couldn't be ignored; and for us – as religious Jews – the ethical problem was that much greater. In a few of them I sensed a considerable shift, but their sense of the 'macho' wouldn't allow them to admit it publicly.

Two years later, in the summer of 1985, the Van Leer Foundation published the results of a survey of six hundred other high school pupils, of the same age as Ms Ben Aharon's, about their attitude towards Arabs and their support for the extreme right-wing Kach party of Meir Kahane. They had not had the opportunity to study To Live Together. Forty-two per cent of the sample gave their support to Kahane's racist policies. And in religious schools he was popular among 59 per cent of all pupils.

I asked her how she felt now about the programme. She was despondent. 'What's the point? I can't teach this when Jews are being murdered by Arabs,' she said. 'At the same time, if we don't do it now, I feel it will be a catastrophe.'

Rivka Ben Aharon works in a religious school because she, like the rest of her family, is an Orthodox Jew. They go to synagogue every Friday night – 'I know that some of those who are extremely religious are also very hostile to the Arabs, but we are not like that.' She has five daughters. 'My husband is an engineer in Jerusalem. He works hard in our home! But so do the girls – today I gave them a list, of what they had to do before I get back home. Tomorrow is Shabat and we have a lot of preparation to do.'

She carries on with the programme in spite of her doubt.

But we must try, no matter what the situation in the street.
My students say, '*They* don't want these studies, do they?
They want hatred' . . . I think it's getting stronger all the
time, on both sides. My brother died in the Yom Kippur war
in 1973. When he was a baby, and my mother held him in
her arms, she used to say to him 'When you are big there will
be peace.' What can I say today to my baby? Nobody
believes in peace while there is terrorism . . . and where does
that come from? I think tragedy comes in a circle.

That question of growing unrest did not seem to be something that Ms Ben Aharon had confronted. I was left with the impression of a caring, thoughtful person who hopes for peace but is not determined on an Israeli compromise. In fact the very opposite. She and her family have recently moved from Jerusalem to the new, raw town of Efrat on the West Bank, south of Bethlehem – yet another of the new developments there that make the likelihood of handing over any part of the territory increasingly remote.

I have many fears about the future – to whom will we belong
in Efrat if they make peace? To Israel or Jordan? Even Rabin

[a Cabinet Minister], who came to Efrat last week, said it would belong to Israel for ever: but we don't know, because we are in the military zone. I know we should give part of Judea and Samaria back, but what? Hardly anyone in Israel thinks we can give back all the area. That is no longer a reality.

It was very good, the small Israel before 1967, but the guns were very close. We are talking of survival. Small Israel was very intimate, but we can't survive on that scale.

Of course there are educational establishments all over Israel, and not just in Jerusalem. At Ulpan Akiva Shulamith Katnelson has a wide variety of short-term students of all ages and with varying degrees of knowledge of Hebrew and Arabic.

We try to listen where their needs are – where their ignorance and where their interests lie – the whole idea of this school is to answer needs.

Now we have those who learn Hebrew, illiterate or writers, and others with no Hebrew: they have been through integration centres, but not for long enough. Newcomer or tourist – they are divided not according to status, just according to the level of Hebrew. So in class you see Ethiopian children with children who are newcomers from other countries, with professors, with musicians, with diplomats. It makes a pluralistic experience.

Every month at least one fourth of the course are Arabs, from Judea and Shomron and Gaza; Druze from the Golan . . . when we entered the Lebanon people could immediately apply to us for a scholarship, and we brought here Druze, Christian, Muslim, and Jews from Lebanon – and when they got stuck there, in misery, we sent them food parcels!

When we had here Tish'a Be'av and we read the Book of Lamentations about the destruction of the two temples in Jerusalem, and how on these temples there is now a mosque, we are praying. Some are praying for a temple and others are not, but we are all praying; the Christians and the Muslims too. You can make this a moment of dispute or you can say

'For heaven's sake, how come God put everything in one
focus, and forces us to look into this focus – and so much
blood in this town of peace? Do we want another
destruction? Can we avoid it?' By hating those Jews who
think differently we don't bring the peace. The second temple
was destroyed because of this . . . let's try to build our small
circle of peace, and the Arabs must sing their songs of
Jerusalem. We didn't sing songs of how we'll conquer
Jerusalem – we spoke of the holiness of the city. And when
we meet together we study together not to dispute, but
Jewish history, Muslim history.

But when she had finished, she added, 'But you must
remember we're not ecumenical. This is a Jewish State and the
Arabs are stuck with us.'

The strong links between education and religion evinced by
Shulamith Katnelson were echoed for me by Pnina Herzog, a
pharmacist and the Ministry of Health's director of international relations. She lives just down the road from her
brother-in-law, the President of Israel. She was born in Tel Aviv
to a rabbinical family that treated its daughters equally with its
sons.

Even if my friends used to come and call me to go and play
or go for a walk, I had to sit with the boys and we had to
learn Jewish studies together. My parents were pharmacists
but both came from rabbinic families and my father was a
learned man of the Talmud. They both worked, and there
was great love and understanding between them. My father
was very good at neglecting the business – he was always
worrying about other people – this one was poor, that one
was ill, you had to help. That's very much in the Jewish
tradition, you know.

Today she believes that:

God has designed Arab and Jew to live side by side in this
region. We must do everything we can to understand each
other and live peacefully together. Sometimes I believe that it
might have happened, if it were not for forces from outside

the country. There were times in the history of Israel when we were quite close to making peace, but there were always forces from without.[3] It's a much broader problem than meets the eye – not one only of the local Arabs and Jews who live here.

I was born in this country: I'm a Palestinian. My brother fell during the war of liberation while he was giving first aid to a wounded friend. He died from an Arab bullet and yet there is no hatred in my heart. Most Israeli Jews have no hatred, only sadness that after so many years we are still in the same position. In spite of all the difficult political ideologies you hear in this country, and there are many – should you give this back, should you give that back – there is only one crucial issue. Do the Palestinians, the PLO, accept Israel as an independent, viable country with whom they will make peace?

All the rest is immaterial. This is the heart of the problem, the main issue. Will they accept us and not want a Palestinian state here in the place of Israel? The moment an Arab state says they want peace one goes to the negotiating table – and there one can start the dialogue; then there are no guns.

Of the many denominations of Orthodox Jewry in Israel, most are ardent supporters of the 40-year-old State. But the Schaimbergers, who live in the most Orthodox heart of Jerusalem, are members of a community hostile to Zionism. If you go into Me'ah She'arim every man – and all the boys, younger and older – wear long black trousers and look pale and languid even when they're playing football. They have skullcaps whose every different colour has a religious or political significance; they wear ringlets where others would cultivate sideburns. For women the street signs are quite explicit – No open collars, No trousers, Cover your arms. I pulled up my collar and pushed greying hair under a headscarf.

---

3 A slightly disingenuous attempt by Pnina Herzog to put all the blame for the lack of peace in the region on other countries, as though Israel, Syria and the others are all just puppets dancing to an American or a Russian tune.

Surely no one would care what I wore? It was difficult to see myself as an object of lust (the biblical reason for covering almost every bit of available skin) but when I met Rabbi Schaimberger and his wife, and their daughter Nechama, he was embarrassed when I put out my hand in greeting, and turned aside. The Rabbi has never touched hands with any woman except his wife, his mother and his sister, to help prevent any dangerous inflammation of feeling.

The Schaimbergers take no holidays and do not leave the crowded, narrow streets where the family has lived for 125 years, ever since they arrived in the city that means more to them than anywhere else in the world.

We met in their small apartment on the first floor of a long and rambling old building that had the look of a former barracks. They have no balcony to help catch a cool evening wind, nowhere to make their lives except the small living room where we sat down – he and I – a bedroom and a tiny kitchen. His black and white pinstriped frockcoat hung on the side of the wardrobe in the room where we talked, where the table had only just been cleared of the remains of their evening meal. Mrs Schaimberger was amused by my question about their relationship – how could it be equal if only he sat? She nodded when he called it a partnership, full of honour and respect, but she did not, herself, add a word to the conversation.

They met before their wedding, but only an hour before the ceremony thirty-eight years ago, and do not seem to have found the lack of prior acquaintanceship a problem. According to custom, the families had discussed the union with some care before they decided the two would be suitable, and the Schaimbergers have done the same – again with success – with their own three children. (But that's not what the Rabbi boasts about, with his gentle smile, when he permits himself a little joke: at the steady religious centre of life, what matters most of all is that his two sons are even more devout, more dedicated, than he. He does not mention his wife, or Nechama, in matters of piety – but he smiles in approbation at the thought that his sons' ringlets are even longer than his own.)

We talk in a lively mixture of German, Yiddish and Hebrew.

Faith is central to the whole family, and it helps determine the women's roles too. Nechama is pregnant with a second child; her mother looks after the first every day so that she can go out to do office work while her husband studies for the rabbinate. Rabbi Schaimberger works in a kosher food hall, earning enough for their daily needs during hours that fit in with twice daily prayer. They have no motor car and I was surprised to see a large, old-fashioned black telephone in the flat.

Rabbi Schaimberger glories in his family and believes in partnership. 'If I had come home and tried to act the boss it wouldn't have worked. All our action is based on joint discussion . . . I honour her more than myself.' Still he sat, talking at the table, while Mrs Schaimberger tidied the kitchen and Nechama attended a tired child. In 1948 they lived on 150 grammes of bread a day while the war – in which they took no part – screamed around them. Their hostility to militarism and Zionism is implacable. In 1967 they were bombed. 'I'm not a coward,' the Rabbi said. 'The Arab Legion were a hundred metres from the flat and I still wouldn't let the Israelis use the flat to defend themselves.'

He had not included Mrs Schaimberger in that statement either, but they were serene and at one together. An hour later I followed them to the nearby synagogue, a large room with a courtyard on one of Me'ah She'arim's narrow and populous streets. There, through open windows, came the sound of prayer and incantation, basso, tenor. Outside, on the pavement, the women strained to hear. They had their prayer books open in front of them and were as attentive and observant as the men. But they wore no black or pinstripe; nor do they enter the synagogue, the House of their Lord.

CHAPTER 4

MARRIAGE AND DIVORCE IN A RELIGIOUS SOCIETY

I walked through the fashionable Jewish suburb of Talpiot in Jerusalem on a summer Saturday in July and passed two young women going in opposite directions – one in a long-sleeved silk blouse, a skirt to mid-calf, midnight blue nylons and stiletto heels, with a large triangle of cloth to cover auburn hair. Swinging past her in impeccable shorts, her only haircovering the headphones and wires of a pocket cassette player clipped to her shirt, came a roller skater with darker curls. There was a flash of disapproval from Miss Stiletto Heels as she circumnavigated round the skater; then she walked quietly on and into the nearby synagogue. Disapproval, yes, but no prohibition as to what is allowed on the Sabbath, even though the shift to the Messianic right and greater religious control of daily life has grown apace in the past ten years. That applies especially to women. With Muslim women, too, the appropriate covering of the flesh, and proper behaviour, is just as strongly a part of local social mechanisms; I would certainly not have seen an Arab roller skater on a Friday or any other day of the week.

Marriage and divorce, for Jewish couples as for Muslim, has been handled by religious authorities since 1953. It is not possible to have a civil wedding in Israel or its dependent territories, and those who wish it leave for a quick ceremony in Cyprus, if they have the money – but they may then fall foul of inheritance laws or welfare rights because the marriage lacks legitimacy. Many conform willingly and do not miss the freedom of a secular State, but there are rebels. Netiva Ben Yehuda's daughter, for example, did not get married until she was seven months pregnant, as her mother relates:

> It was not in the synagogue . . . first of all they live together
> for a very long time and she was already in the seventh
> month pregnant. My father and mother used to phone her
> day and night, every minute with another argument why they
> should get married. So in the end they decided to give my
> parents a present, and they brought a rabbi to their
> apartment.
>
> He was very, you know, on the defensive when he came,
> because they are both hippies. Also she had not been for the
> ritual bath, she had not been to the Mikve (how could she,
> her stomach so big already?). We were afraid he would not
> do it, that he would start a fight because they were
> hippies – I was ready to pay for them to buy a ticket to go to
> Cyprus, but he took his money, the Rabbi, and he married
> them.

Judy Levitan, who lives in Jerusalem, was upset about her
lack of choice: she feels passionately about the right to choose.

> The only way you can legally marry is with a religious
> ceremony. You go to the Rabbinate – it's a state institute:
> there they ask you a lot of questions, and they give you a lot
> of lectures about how you should behave before marriage
> and after marriage, what you should do with your husband;
> you should start lighting candles on a Friday evening. You
> have to say Yes, Yes, otherwise you get into complications.
> Then you have to have the ritual cleansing in the Mikve the
> night before your wedding. Often you have to tell them lies,
> because the cleansing is supposed to come a few days after
> the end of your period, and plans and dates go wrong. If the
> wedding falls during the days when you are still not regarded
> as 'clean', you go there and you work out beforehand how to
> make it seem okay, otherwise you'd have to scrap the
> wedding day!
>
> I resented all this very much: I had the feeling I wanted to
> strike some of the stupid religious people who were sitting
> around at the Institute . . . but of course I didn't. I went, like

a good little child, sat there and had to listen to all this
rubbish because I knew that I had to go through with it if I
wanted to be married. I did make one mistake: I began to
argue with them. It took one and a half hours, whereas
Chananiah [her fiancé] was only in there ten minutes. They
were trying to persuade me to be religious . . . I resented that
very much, because of course by law I had to be there.
It implies that the State, more and more, restricts my rights
as a human being. I'm sort of, an extension of the State,
instead of the State being a framework where I can choose
my own way of life.
Everything in Israel is turned upside down. It's like living in a
nightmare; it's also illogical, quite against what we have been
brought up to . . . we're going backwards, away from
democracy . . . we in Israel tried to imitate the modern
world, Britain and the States, other countries; we didn't try
to imitate the under-developed world. Sometimes I feel Israel
is becoming like Uganda, or like Kuwait, where they cut
people's hands because they have stolen. It's going to happen
in Israel, if present trends go on . . . where's the limit? A lot
of people want the Halacha[1] to be the law of the country.
Can you imagine?
    The Halacha was written more than a thousand years
ago – how can it possibly be democratic? It was built up in a
quite different society, with different needs and outlooks.
Judaism has always been an excluding factor for the Arabs,
for their possibility of integrating into the area.
Judaism – everyone who is not Jewish cannot have the same
status as a Jew. That's something you can't do anything
about, like being white or black. But it's also excluding for
the non-religious people, for the secular ones like me. It's got
to the point here that *every* Gentile is unacceptable, whether

1 Halacha. The body of Jewish religious doctrine that determines marriage,
divorce, illegitimacy and maintenance practice. It is administered by all male
rabbinical courts which have been shown to favour the man in any dispute
and the laws themselves are biased towards the man. For example, men are
allowed to marry a second time if their wife is mentally ill, even when there
has been no divorce, but women are not.

they're Arab or Christian. People say things like 'We don't want democracy, because democracy isn't Jewish' . . . they go to that extreme.

The people in the new settlements on the West Bank especially are developing this new kind of religiosity: it wasn't part of Israeli society in the past, this kind of attitude . . . they're awaiting the Messiah, and while they wait we all have to be a gathering of the holy. Anything which is not Jewish is out of the question, for them.

In fact, although according to Halacha a Jew may marry only a Jew, it is possible to undergo a conversion, for someone really determined and committed. Pnina Herzog, with a strongly religious background, does not believe a civil wedding ceremony would be helpful to the situation of Jews in Israel.

I am absolutely against introducing civil marriage in this country. Today, no matter whether you are religious or secular, young people can marry each other even if one is religious and the other is not. They get married by the one marriage ceremony that exists, and so we are one people, we are one nation no matter what our beliefs are. Ben-Gurion,[2] who was an absolutely secular man, realised this and said he would not introduce civil marriage. It would create in your own people, your own country, two groups of people . . .

The traditional ceremony is a very simple ceremony; it's not offensive to anyone. It is enough to have two witnesses, and one says the accepted words: 'You are hereby made holy to me' . . . according to Jewish law, you are married. So I don't see it as coercion. It's not offensive, and it helps preserve the Jewish nation.

We do certain things so as not to break up the nation – today we are so small that we must do everything we can to preserve the wholeness of our people.

---

2 David Ben-Gurion: an early Zionist leader who became the first Prime Minister of Israel in 1948. One of the major architects of the new State, he was the leader of the Labour coalition. He was replaced by Golda Meir in August 1969.

Among Muslim women there are many arranged marriages, as among ultra-Orthodox Jewish women, and overall they marry young. Child brides have been outlawed but most marry between 17 and 21: by their mid twenties, three or four children is not unusual. Polygyny, too, although frowned on by State and official religion, is not uncommon, especially among Bedouin people. Less than 5 percent of women never marry. Many, through ignorance, male hostility or poverty, do not seek available contraception. Legally, it is only possible to apply for an abortion if one is under 17 or over 40 or there is danger to life, but the pressure to bear many children is great. Among young unmarried Muslim women, too, there is strong moral and family censure of unmarried pregnancy and 'family honour' murders still occur regularly.

Esther Elliam has a grown-up family.

To keep the religious groups happy people pay high prices for back street abortions: that keeps the gynaecologists happy too! I'm 46 and I had an abortion six months ago. The gynaecologist told me I was pregnant, and then he said 'Mazeltov' [Good fortune]. No, I said, not Mazeltov, I want to have an abortion. He stared at me as though I'm committing a crime! He questioned me: 'What's the matter? Why do you want an abortion?' He would certainly not have told me what my rights were – an ignorant woman would never have got her abortion. I got mine, but I had to be very assertive; it was really unbearable.

It could also have been dangerous for me, at my age, and the child could have been a mongol. But the pressure to have children here is so great – just as strong among Arabs as Jews: everyone is busy counting to see which can be the larger population by the twenty-first century! Policy on abortion is not only controlled by the religious bodies – politics is in it as well.

Many women do use contraception, but they're not always taught to handle it in the proper way. The IUD is the most popular, but often proper care isn't taken and it's left in for months or years, making a terrible inflammation. It's all part of the secrecy: secrecy from their husbands, secrecy because we're all supposed to want more and more children, more and more to cover this pocket handkerchief of a place . . .

Carmit Gie corroborated Esther's views.

In marriage very Orthodox Jews don't use contraceptives: procreation is a virtue – the more kids you have the better. And in Israel it's combined with the kind of military society we live in. In the early 1950s, children were going to be our future Army, so large families had extra benefits . . . they still do. So religious couples don't use contraceptives: a professor who deals with infertility problems told me that if the Orthodox women don't conceive within a year of marriage they're in deep trouble, from the family and the surrounding society.

On the other hand the rules are very strict about when they have intercourse; the prohibition is not only during the period but also for the first week after it has come to an end. And sperm tests are not allowed on the husbands because masturbation is a sin in Jewish law, the sin of Onan. A man may not spill his seed, nor is artificial insemination allowed. None of the special techniques that we have developed against infertility can be used, while at the same time true Orthodoxy means a child a year – at 25 there'll already be four or five kids running after her.

We're continually being told that we are so few and the Arabs so many – the way to do something about it, when not many Jews come from abroad, is to have more and more babies. Nationalism and Orthodoxy come together here, as so often.

Among Muslim women contraception as a practice is growing gradually. At marriage, a woman receives a dowry which is regarded as her future safeguard in case she is widowed or divorced. Her husband has a duty to provide for her and any children, but on his death she receives, on average, only a half the inheritance of any male heirs.

Hiam Abbass comes from Deir Hanna in Galilee. Now in her

mid-twenties, she recently married an Englishman, Michael
Allan.

My parents are no different from other parents in a
Palestinian village. They had a bit more education, that's all.
It made going out of the village much easier for me, I should
think, than for other women: and then it was just the
opening of my new style of life.

I went to Haifa to study photography and I started to see
things differently from other women in the village, seeing my
life as an independent woman in a different way. I wanted to
struggle alone and be independent from my parents, and
from the authority that men held in the village.

It was very difficult, not easy at all. I quarrelled with my
parents many times and there were long times when I did not
return home. They saw me as something strange, something
different, but they did not know how to explain it to
themselves. They did not want to understand and they tried
to stop me many times. Sometimes my mother tried to
convince my father to let me continue my studies – she began
to understand me, slowly, because I kept in contact with her
much more than with my father. I found it impossible to
speak to him.

After a long time I decided to marry Michael, and today
there are still many people in the village with whom I do not
have contact, just for that. But I decided to convince my
parents I was doing something right; I did not want to act in
an isolated way – I struggled to the last minute, until they
agreed. It took two years!

In the beginning it was very difficult for them to
understand why I, as a Muslim, should not marry a Muslim
and a Palestinian. But slowly my mother got used to the idea;
she knew that this is what I wanted and that nothing could
change my mind. She helped me a lot in convincing my
father; many times I came home and told him, 'You have
two choices – between your old society and your daughter.'
In the end he just had to agree.

Michael became a Muslim in order to get married here in

Israel, so that we could do it with my parents. It was the only way we could make it in this country: he had to become a Muslim to be able to make a contract. People in the village could not believe it, many Palestinians don't! They just keep asking and asking again and again, just to make sure it's true; and they look at my hand to see the ring. They say, 'Why did you marry a foreigner; aren't there enough Muslim people to marry?'

I want to have a family later on, not now. I don't see myself as having children yet because I want to give time to children. I think in all religions women are seen as inferior to men, the Muslim as any other, but that is not the way Michael and I do things – nor will we change when we have children.

We were always known as the educated family in the village and therefore people expected a lot from us as women. My mother was a teacher, like my father, and when she worked she was really independent. She never cooked I remember my grandmother did the cooking – and my father used to put the food on the table (that's unheard of among Muslims!) and eat alone. If he had anything wrong with his clothes, he would fix it. But suddenly, when she stopped teaching, she became like any other woman in the village.

As soon as she stopped teaching she just started working in the house, meeting women, bringing up children – and my father immediately stopped doing anything at all. He did things all those years because he had no choice – she really didn't have the time. But not he, and certainly not she, had changed: they just went back to the old ways.

That will never happen to me.

The Koran gives the man the right to decide if he wants a divorce: 'Divorce must be pronounced twice and then a woman must be retained in honor or released in kindness.' (2: 229) He can take her back, after reflection, and she has the right to go to arbitration with representatives of his family and her family, but there is no question of equal rights. Divorce figures are low, but the bitterness and anger felt by abandoned wives is as great as that felt by Jewish women in a similar situation.

Haya Hadad went to Israel from Djerba in Tunisia in 1949 as a child of 11. When she was 18 she married her cousin Amos, who had also come from Tunisia, and they moved into a small flat that her parents helped them buy. Amos became a teacher and they had six children – by this time living in a bigger home in Kiryat Gat in the northern Negev. Amos became deputy mayor and was active on the local religious council.

At first everything was wonderful, says Haya.

> I was the first woman in the neighbourhood to have a telephone and I had a cleaning woman too. We went on vacations all over the country. The trouble began when Amos came home late one day and supper wasn't ready. He threw a hot plate at me – and that's when I had my first and only epileptic fit.

A year later he introduced Hanna to the family (he described her as his secretary).

> From that moment she was with us everywhere. When we went to the movies, when we went on vacation and when we celebrated festivals. Hanna and her mother and her relatives were always with us.

Haya Hadad refused a divorce but in 1978 the rabbinical court gave Amos permission to take a second wife because she was epileptic. He sold their home (and she discovered that the house had been in his name only and that she had no rights although they had shared it for so many years) and bought a small flat for her use, but in a son's name. Haya is bitter and sad. She feels she has become a 'throwaway wife' after twenty years during which she was 'good enough' to have six children. She feels powerless and discriminated against. Her husband has become a government representative in New York.

Unless both man and woman agree, divorcing couples who are Jewish cannot go to a secular court, but at least a woman has enough independence to be able to initiate the separation proceedings in that court, as well as under rabbinical administration. But then Jewish women are exposed to the lack of natural justice favoured by the Rabbinate. According to a survey by Na'amat, the largest women's organisation in Israel, those who can go to the civil court to ask for maintenance or alimony receive, on average, twice the number of shekels each month as those in the law of religion. In addition, if a man does not agree to a divorce, the law of the Torah cannot force him to it, as it can a woman: he can be fined or gaoled under civil procedures but his wife will never get the decree nisi. Increasingly, too, the figures in recent years show fathers getting custody of their children unless they are very young. The Rabbis have even, in a reversion to ancient polygynous custom, enabled a man to take a second wife if his first partner has refused the divorce.

'The poor woman fell ill and grew old and it is obvious that his eyes and his heart cannot allow him to live with her as husband and wife,' said a recent rabbinical judgment about 56-year-old Rachel, who had started her married life thirty years earlier on a Hashomer Hatzair kibbutz hostile to religious practice. 'She is repulsive in his eyes and must be divorced. She is old beyond repair.' Rachel had refused to grant the Get or divorce that her husband had demanded. As a result of the judgment he was able to marry again without the Get, leaving her homeless and with no maintenance. (The Rabbis had also noted, at length, that there had been 'only' daughters from the union, whereas to be fruitful and multiply is interpreted to mean at least one son and one daughter.) In similar circumstances, the wife cannot take a second husband without being seen as adulterous and a fallen woman, producing bastards.

The broadcaster Carmit Gie has met women seeking a legal separation in the course of her work in news and current affairs.

There are several hundred women in Israel who cannot get their divorce. They have marched through the streets of Jerusalem this week, and I spoke to two of them. One has been fighting for twenty-two years and has been unable to do anything, because when she first started the procedures her attorney told her to leave the house. That was a major mistake – she was immediately deprived of all her rights, even though she had left the house after being physically very badly treated by the husband. Her six months old baby was also molested. Since then he has said No to a divorce, and that's it . . .

The other has been struggling for her divorce for eleven years. She helped form a lobby to try and solve the problems. They've met with the Chief Rabbis and with several authorities on Halacha and they say that the rabbis, in recent years, have become far more extreme, and less sympathetic to the woman in each case. They don't co-operate: they only want to make things worse for the woman. So that's why they demonstrated outside the offices of the Rabbinate in Tel Aviv – there were at least five hundred women there.

There are several refuges for battered women in Israel, in spite of the enormous problems that arise when a married woman leaves her own home . . . a friend of mine went to the refuge in Herzelia after she came out of hospital – she'd had a really severe beating up by her husband. But it doesn't help the women solve their major life's problems, especially if they have young children and don't want to go straight back to work.

The only way marriage really works for Jewish women here is when it's happy! We are our husband's property . . . even though I earn more than Eli, I'm still the 'second' wage earner.

I'm his property even at Kupat Holim, at the health service. A friend of mine had been travelling abroad. She came back to Israel with their four children, a month ahead of her husband, and tried to renew their health insurance. They said 'No, you will have to wait for him.' She asked what would happen if one of them was ill in the meantime – kids fall ill all the time, don't they? – and was told there was nothing she could do. She did not exist as an independent entity without her husband.

Sima Waxman is a Sabra who went to live in Canada with

her husband and daughter Mia. He left her and she decided to return to Israel; he had said he would not oppose a divorce and she did not expect any difficulties, but when she got home life was far more difficult than she had expected.

When Mia and I first arrived no one would rent an apartment to us because I was divorcing: the stigma of the divorced woman was already mine. That was in 1979. I had signed a contract for an apartment, and was supposed to come back the same evening to pick up the key. When I arrived at the lawyer's office he suddenly pretended he never saw me in his life before . . . he must have told his client I was divorcing. Here the stigma was also about the chance that I might take a different man to the apartment every night!
    They think that a woman who has been married, with a regular relationship with a man, still has the need once the couple break up. They think you'll just take any man! I was very upset, and I didn't have any other place to stay. It took me weeks to get an apartment.
    There's an expression in Hebrew – Aguna – which means a deserted mother. My husband and I were separated seven years ago, and I was able to get a divorce only last year. The situation was difficult because in Jewish law I was still a married woman; obviously I wasn't – but was I Aguna? I wasn't with the man, yet when I needed any help from the government, like getting a loan for a house, I couldn't get it because I was still registered as married. In the case of wanting to buy a house it means the man has to come and sign in order to get the loan because it's a programme for young couples. I was in trouble all the time – I couldn't get a passport either, or write Mia down in the passport, because I needed my former husband's signature. He had moved to New York and didn't really exist for me, or for Mia, any longer.
    I get no alimony from him either. Last year, after such a time, I finally went to court and pressed charges against him . . . I won, but only a very small monthly amount. I

think they gave it to me just to shut my mouth! The money comes from social security because they can't find him, and they send letters to America to try and make him pay back.

Imagine – it took seven years to get that divorce, because of our religious laws. Even though my husband had left me, I was called shameful, as though I had left him: that's the way they treated me. I was not a good woman. Once, after five years, they found him somewhere in Vancouver and he signed the Get (divorce) papers. But when they sent a telegram from the rabbis in New York to the rabbis in Jerusalem they made one mistake in the spelling of my name: that was against the rabbinical law. So they had to start again – it had to go back, and it took a few more years. I had to pay a lot of money: the rabbis in New York told the Rabbinate here 'Listen, people, you make mitzvas in Israel, good deeds – and in New York we make business.' Seven years! It took until last May.

If Sima had been Christian, Druze or Muslim, the Israeli law on desertion would finally have come to her aid because non-Jews can remarry after seven years, the assumption being – after such a biblical span – they are now single again.

The difficulties of women who wish to divorce, or do not want to divorce, or who are left in a parlous financial state, are centrally linked to religious custom and practice. At the same time the fact that women are the second sex in earning and as holders of power compounds marriage and divorce inequities. During marriage a Jewish man may have as many adulterous relationships as he wishes; a woman may not. But he also usually comes home with more money in his pocket and he is often the prime decision maker. It is women who bear the brunt of the burden when he changes his mind and wants out, and paradoxically, if she makes the first move, she still has more to bear. Both Muslim and Jewish women find, after divorce, that they have lost status and money. No law exists about the equal sharing of the major asset – the matrimonial home.

Judy Levitan has the final word:

The Jewish religion was never against divorce as much as, say, the Catholics. But even within marriage the status of the woman is too low. When there's a divorce, and the husband wants the children, he has only to wear a kippa on his head for two weeks and go to the Yeshiva. Then automatically he says 'My wife is not religious, and I am' – and as it's a religious court he gets custody of the children. She is left with nothing in her hands . . .

CHAPTER 5

OF PECKING ORDERS
AND POVERTY

> Jews from Morocco have no education. Their
> customs are those of Arabs. They love their
> wives but they beat them.
> *Prime Minister David Ben-Gurion in 1965*

Vera Foltys and Nitza Ben Zvi sat discussing the employment
situation of women in Israel amicably. They were old friends
and often collaborated. Vera is in charge of the section that
deals with work, benefits and training courses for women at her
employment exchange; Nitza – though not with relish – is
Israel's chief civil servant with responsibility for women's work.
Her tiny, crowded office in a large building opposite the
Knesset in Jerusalem has a picture of Shimon Peres on the wall,
an ever open door and great cluttered friendliness. I found a
space in which to sit down and they began to tell me about the
difficulties of working women. They need shorter hours; they
would not work on Shabat (Saturday) if they were in the
catering trade; they did not apply for promotion that would
entail travelling, extra responsibility or evening meetings.

The 38 per cent of women who are at work try to tailor their
jobs to their families: Vera and Nitza said that, except for those
employed as academics, most women had given up all thought
of equal standing with men. 'If they ever had it in the first
place' said Nitza, who has spent years arranging courses,
encouraging women in the civil service, pushing for equality:
she has become weary.

We had talked for half an hour and I asked about work for Arab women; somehow, as so often, it didn't automatically appear on the agenda. Nitza said, 'Not many go out to work' and we went on to talk of women's traditional choices – typing, confectionery work, low-level electronics, teaching (with the glorious statistic that 80 per cent of all teachers are women but 80 per cent of all head teachers are . . . men, in spite of their regular Army service; during those months women are good enough to stand in for them).

Again I asked about Arab women; again we slid rapidly away: they were really not part of the everyday problems. Was this because less than half as many Arab women – 17 per cent – worked, compared with their Jewish sisters? At my third try Nitza became specific – yes, economic need was pushing younger women into the labour market, but often, when they left home, they were put in the charge of a minder by the father and could go off only to group work in the fields or a factory. Married women usually stopped work other than agriculture, teaching or nursing. Oh, hairdressing was becoming a popular trade for Arab women.

We spent an hour together, and then I went with Vera to the labour exchange where she worked. She introduced me to 40-year-old Alisa who had come to Israel in 1953 from Fez in Morocco. Alisa has five children between the ages of 5 and 17. She is eager to work but her husband, who is a carpenter, forbids her to work on the Sabbath, so she had just lost a job in an old people's home. Alisa is prepared to do anything – she has worked in the textile industry, as a hairdresser and in a kindergarten.

Raisa Shlemyaf, who is 50, came to Israel from the Soviet Union. She is a good cook and says that the best thing she does is borscht (beetroot soup). She has been working a six-day week in an Army hostel that has now shut: as she has two daughters at home she does not want to take on the even more arduous hours of hotel work. She is joined by Tziona Moaleb, who came to Israel from Syria when she was 21. Tziona has had only three years' schooling because all Jewish schools were closed by the Syrian government while she was a pupil. She has worked as a cook and as a hotel supervisor; she looks after her mother, who is 85. Tziona is bitter: she refused a temporary job and has had her unemployment benefit suspended for a month.

There were no Arab women at the labour exchange but the women I met were nearly all Sephardi or Oriental Jews who had emigrated to Israel in the early 1950s when Israel's major population boom took place, mostly from other Middle Eastern or North African countries. Sephardi people are traditionally lower in the Israeli social order, and frequently earn less money than their Ashkenazi counterparts who came from Europe. They resent the stranglehold that European Jews had on power bases in industry, the government and trade unions until 1978 and the first Likud administration, but they themselves often display the same kind of arrogance that informs the statement of former Prime Minister Ben Gurion at the beginning of this chapter. I went on to talk with Sima Waxman, who sees herself as Sephardi.

I was born in Jerusalem, but I'm known as a Moroccan Jewess. I was born here, in Baca. I feel myself to be Moroccan, since that's the way I was brought up – it's the basic culture that I've got. Why do they call me Moroccan? In order to make the difference between Ashkenazi and Sephardi. The Ashkenazi Jews see themselves as above us, as above the Sephardi. It's not what I think, but I don't think the opposite either; they are really arrogant. I've always lived among Ashkenazis and Sephardis: I'm really aware of the problem.

I'm involved because I'm a Moroccan and I think that my culture, and the way I was brought up, has a lot to give and a lot for others to learn. It's the closeness in the family, and the warmth and the touching, which I think a lot of Ashkenazis don't know. And discrimination – Ashkenazis are bad at that. After living for eight years overseas, I came back to Israel just when my daughter was ready to go to school: since I didn't have an address at that time, I had the privilege of choosing a school.

So I chose a school that seemed good, and I went there to

register her. I had never had problems with being a Moroccan. I went in, and the secretary asked me my names. I said Sima Waxman, and then she looked at me and she said, 'She's so fair, and you're so dark.' Then she said to me, 'Where did your parents come from?' And I told her, 'I don't think I have to answer you. When my parents went to register me in school, nobody asked them where their parents came from.' And I said, 'Thank you, no, I really, really would be very happy if my daughter didn't study in your school.'

Now she studies here in Baca, in the community school, and it has everything – they do still ask 'Where do you come from', but they're not snobbish like that other school. Mia says she's part of this and part of that . . . as Sabras we really have to get away from these awful feelings that one kind is better than another kind.

There is hostility between Ashkenazi and Sephardi still today – there's hostility and snobbishness from both sides. I think it's got worse in some ways in the past ten years. But at the same time we're also starting to see some changes within the Jewish community – not only hostility. You can hear it in the music you didn't hear before: there's a lot of Middle Eastern music sung by Sephardis and Ashkenazis. It's contradictory: there's a lot of neighbourhood hostility . . . at the same time it's making a richer culture – Jews from Morocco, from Yemen, from Poland, from Russia . . . but there are many difficulties. [The music that I heard in Baca had a strong Eastern feel – drums, flutes, lyres and tambourines accompanying high-pitched and, to me, quite monotonous cadences. Ed.]

For me the hostility between Jew and Arab is exactly the same thing as the hostility between Jew and Jew. I don't have any problem with my identity or with the identity of others – it's the same with Arabs. I mean, first of all they are human beings . . . the way I look at them: if he's a child, that he has a mother and a father, with needs like me or my daughter. It makes no difference to me to treat nicely Ashkenazi or Arab, for that matter.

My daughter was brought up in Canada: she came here

when she was 7, and she didn't speak Hebrew. A few months after she was going to school she started to build up that fear, that stigma towards an Arab, the way he looks, the way he walks – we have to hate them, and stuff like that. I have quite a lot of friends who are Arab; a lot of them Israeli Arabs from before the 1967 war and some of them from now. It was Easter time, and we were invited to a beautiful village in Galilee, to an Arab family – Arab Christians. It was a big house, the grandmother and grandfather and maybe four children who are married, all around them. There was a girl of Mia's age: she realised then that they were no different. The little girl cries if she doesn't like something. She has to go and wash her hands before she sits to eat; she sleeps on a clean sheet when she goes to bed. She talks to her mother and father and she gets kisses just like Mia. It was the first time she had been able to comprehend it.

It is still very important to her to know who is Jew and who is Arab, but we have a lot of Arab friends. This is not unusual for me, and it was never unusual at my family's house. But it is difficult for most people in Israel to be friendly with Arabs. I have a friend who works with me in a community centre, who has a very strong point of view about Arabs – very negative. He voted for Kahane. But since he became my friend he started to see things differently. He told me after two or three months that he was starting to understand, to relate, to react; and not to blame all the time.

In Baca we're a very cosmopolitan part of Jerusalem, with Arab and Jew, Sephardi and Ashkenazi. It's really very unusual in Israel today to have everybody so mixed up. In Baca we'd like some kind of agreement – for instance that Jerusalem will be international territory and we continue to live among them, and they among us, but I don't think we have a majority!

I get no State support of any kind except the tiny sum from the welfare that they try to get back from my husband. I've got two jobs – twice a week I'm a waitress; the rest of the time a community worker. I work with young people and I have a club for mothers with young children. We have a programme for mothers here in Baca, all together once a week. When I first met them it took me about seven months to organise the club. I went from one house to another, and I went especially to homes where I knew there were difficulties; for mothers just to go out and maybe have a coffee. Just leave the laundry and the dishes: I'd pick them all up and we just started to have some fun.

For many of them, it was a first opportunity to get out of the house, and to have contact. They began looking different, week by week. And they had their own ideas; they began doing the cleaning the day before, doing the shopping the next day, to be sure they had the day free. It gives them a lot, and we've also arranged a nursery during the hours we are occupied together, so that they don't have that burden while they enjoy themselves.

I came back to Jerusalem after eight years just to visit with my daughter, for Passover. After the 1967 war people began behaving as though they were living on a different planet – with the victory they stopped thinking for even a moment about the future. Before 1967 people made far greater attempts to live peacefully with the Arabs here; afterwards they didn't care any more, they were so full of themselves. I think that's when the hatred really got worse.

When I came back I didn't plan to stay, but I liked it all of a sudden. I came here and my attitude was different: it's not that I thought differently, but I lived with peace in myself. I thought I can't correct the whole world, but whoever I can correct next to me – that would be just as good as correcting everything else.

I met Miriam and Sara in the marketplace where they were organising their baskets of produce for sale. They enjoyed talking to me: they were frank, but slightly apprehensive because their private sale of moshav produce is against the rules, and especially now when the moshavim generally are undergoing profound economic difficulties. Miriam and Sara, mother and daughter, were in their usual place, among friends and a noisy, cheerful crosscurrent of talk and shouting.

Miriam was born in the Yemen, where she lived a very confined and dependent existence, the men doing even the shopping for cloth and women's clothes. Here Sara translates for her.

My life has been hard; yes, it has been very hard. When the government in Yemen said we had to leave, we walked for many days to go to Aden, so that we could fly here. And do you know what they did when our plane landed? They sprayed us with DDT! Not just the aeroplane – they sprayed *us* . . . how dare they do that thing to us, as though we were dirty?

When we still lived in Yemen we women stayed in the house all the time except when we went to fetch the water, or when we went to visit our friends. We were very poor and nobody went to school – they would not let us. I could not read or write and I spoke Arabic all the time. It was the men who could speak and read the Hebrew, and they taught the boys, but we learnt nothing. We did not go to synagogue either. We only went to the well and to the houses of our friends. At the well we talked to the Arab women as well.

Yemen – it was cruel, but we were used to it. What else did we know? I was married the first time when I was 12, but I ran away. This husband here on the moshav I took in Yemen when I was 18. When we were there so many children died but here it is much better. In Yemen we could not do what we wished. Yes, the men were allowed to work, but only with weaving, that's why we were so poor. We were not allowed to make a school.

Here in Israel I think I'm much happier than my man. You see, he stays on the moshav all the time. It is like he is afraid to go out: he just sits there when he is not working or at the synagogue. For me it is different: I like very much to come here and see my friends – some of them I know for nearly thirty years! Yes, I am selling my own vegetables: we are supposed to give the money to the moshav, but, you know, it is very useful to have a little bit extra. The men keep the rules, but we don't always do like the men . . . yes, I am happy here, but he is not.

Here Sara, who is in her early thirties, took over the story.

Well, I grew up here . . . my family lived in Yemen for many hundred years. It is true what my mother says, I remember my father to be very unhappy when I was a little girl; even now I would not say that he was truly happy. He goes to the synagogue, but otherwise he just sits at home. He was much happier in Yemen, where they said the Torah while they did their weaving. When he came here he thought that at last we would be rich and not poor – that is not possible here on the moshav. He does not like to be a farmer . . . I think he would like best of all to make a business.

My own life? I left the school quite early – I could not see what to stay for. Of course I can read and write, I can do the money sums. I am married to a man from the moshav – we all come from Yemen there, so we understand each other. My parents fixed the marriage and it's quite all right. But I don't want my daughter to live on the moshav: it would be good if we could find a man with a business, in town. You know, life is much more interesting in the town. I spend a lot of money on her, on Rachel . . . today she wants some new shoes with high heels. It will be a matter of how much we sell today!

Oh yes, I'm happy we came here. My mother and father talk still about Yemen – it was not good. I can do more here. Also, there, so many children died: we know better how to do that now. But we still keep the proper ideas. I do not argue with my man, or my father. Mind you, we don't always tell them how much we make here in the market! It helps very much for nice clothes and other things . . . really, Rachel asks for something new every day. If only we can find a nice boy with an apartment in Jerusalem . . . that's where I would like to live as well . . .

I do think our Jewish custom is the right one: the man should be in charge, even if he doesn't always know what we are doing. Can they do what they want on the moshav? Never. The government, and all those other people they send to the moshav: *they* make the rules and *they* decide what is to be done, really, not my father or my man.

Please, please, you must not say who we are and where we do this selling!

Miriam, Sara and Rachel are fictitious names. Neither mother nor daughter showed any interest, in our discussion, in trying to take part in the formal affairs of their moshav (the national average for such participation by women, in the moshavim based on immigrants from Muslim countries, is minute, far smaller than those settled with immigrants from Europe). They did not appear to be concerned about the future, either, although the instances of widows and divorcees who have been forced to leave the moshav or cede all inheritance of their portion to male children,[1] are well documented. Miriam and Sara felt that at least some of their strength came from this regular but informal dealing at the market: they found it enjoyable and satisfying. Their future hopes were pinned on Rachel, and the good life they predicted could be negotiated for her; in the meantime, their own sense of self-esteem was fulfilled. They did not seek any other power base.

The Bedouin women whom I met in the Negev near Beersheva, hold even less power.

At eight o'clock in the morning the midsummer heat of the Negev desert is still bearable. The Bedouin community worker, Sayyid Alsaana, and the Jewish American nurse Varda Burston were talking boisterously together in the front of the van that was to take us from one Bedouin family to another, as part of the twice-weekly journey in their mobile clinic. At first I was more interested in Varda and Sayyid than infant mortality: my experiences in Tel Aviv (where fingers had been snapped for the Arab hotel porter; the receptionist hadn't spoken a word to him) and elsewhere had left me bruised. I ached from moments like that, and was the more curious to see how Sayyid and Varda got on.

One mobile clinic can't do an enormous amount for the

1 For inheritance on the moshavim – see *Ideological Change of Rural Women's Role and Status; a Case Study of Family Based Cooperative Villages in Israel* by Naomi Nevo and David Solomonica of the Jewish Agency, Rehovot, Israel (Jan 1983).

50,000 Bedouin of the Negev. It attracts foreign funding, although none from Israel, and interacts closely with the Beersheva teaching hospital and with mother and baby clinics on its wide-ranging route to help achieve some minor miracles. Dialysis from a tent pole, working on gravity; Ilgrenahle Eisna at home only weeks after open heart surgery, being helped by her husband's first wife although not by him; another woman taught to suck and clear her son's open windpipe – there was a robust approach to medical care on the spot that was inventive and frequently successful.

Varda and Sayyid spoke voluble Bedouin with each other; their relationship was one of close professional trust. It became clear that neither could have done the work without the other: he far more experienced and knowledgeable about local communities and customs, as well as the traits of individual family members; she providing skilled and thoughtful nursing care and advice. They discussed, resolved, and worked as a team, sharing the responsibility of decision-making.

The Negev is bumpy and bare. Or, suddenly, full of fertile wheat fields, some of them Bedouin owned. The Bedouin, with their winglike winter and summer tents, have been under official pressure – at times reinforced with rifle butts – to move into permanent housing for many years but since the Israeli withdrawal from Sinai in 1982 the pressure has been stepped up. The Air Force and military installations in the Negev desert, and the much talked of presence of nuclear plants, has made the demand more urgent: nomadic families and tribes on land they once owned, which they know intimately, has become an impossible embarrassment when there are nuclear secrets to hide. There are new homes in areas designated by the government, in rough concrete and cement, mostly on stilts so that the cooking can still be done in the open under the house, and others with carefully swept yards planted with flowers and vegetables on their perimeter, but with the scoured metal cooking pots still outside, neatly stacked next to a traditional cooking tent.

Then, in the stillness of a midday heat that I was finding difficult to handle, we came to the latest modern innovation – a roof standing on its own, and houses made of the shining silver of corrugated iron. The metal was so hot that it sizzled the fingers to an accidental touch, yet a large group of men and women, veiled and hooded and all in black or white, sat closely together under that blazing cover.

They were quite still and even the children were as stone.

'This roof, and the huts made like them, scald in summer and yet are so cold in winter that our babies get hypothermia.' Varda and Sayyid wish that people would go on using skin tents with brush insulation in the winter and the cool cloth ones of summer, but the impetus towards permanent housing (the plot is lost if not built on within three years) makes that an unreal hope.

We visited Ilgrenahle Eisna. After her recent open heart surgery her elderly husband had been hostile rather than supportive, to the extent that when she had had a relapse at home he hadn't even called the hospital. He had married her for the attributes that a second, much younger wife would bring to his old age – 'Now he sees her as damaged goods,' Varda says. Ilgrenahle is beaming: she knows that without the mobile clinic she would not have survived the last few weeks.

We sit on rugs on the shaded verandah to eat watermelon together; the two wives are friendly and I wonder whether their husband will, after all, achieve the peaceful old age he wants . . . Ilgrenahle's mother has the lines of tattooing on her face and her hair is henna orange, put into wispy plaits. We all enjoy ourselves – the mother is especially attentive to Sayyid and Varda, offering food, a cool drink and cold water to splash on face and hands.

Bedouin men, like the Druze but unlike all other Arabs, can serve in the Army: that means that welfare benefits for the children are higher, but the malnutrition diseases of kwashiorkor and marasmus are abundant in the desert today. Before 1948, with plenty of land, the Bedouin grew figs, olives, squash, okra and tomatoes. Today, uprooted and resettled, infant mortality figures are still too high and Sayyid shakes his head when he talks of them. Today, he and Varda encourage families to grow fresh produce again. Many babies are small and not thriving properly.

We continue along dirt roads, past isolated houses and shacks and go into small villages. In that heat, women minding the flocks all wear black enveloping head shawls so that they can be seen at a distance by men; white would be far cooler but is only allowed indoors. Young Bedouin women do not go out to work except as shepherds, and even those who mind the fat-tailed woolly sheep out on the wide horizons live under the dependency of male control. In Beersheva's Thursday market, there are Bedouin women minding a stall here and there, but it's a very small omen.

Back in Beersheva, where 14-year-old Abuish has just had her stomach pumped clear of the petrol she had swallowed that morning, the emphasis is suddenly on transition and rebellion. Abuish swallowed the petrol because she could no longer bear the beatings from her father; she said she would rather die. When she came round, she also proposed to move out – quite unheard of in the present framework of paternal control.

Before our return Varda had shown me a hole in the ground where insulin was being kept cool with wet leaves that were continually dampened. She said:

We certainly don't see 50,000 people . . . there is also a mobile vaccination clinic and a couple that look after babies. We spend 70 per cent of our time with children – follow up care of children who have been in hospital, and quite a bit of that is gastro-enteritis follow-up care and teaching hygiene and nutrition.

There's a great deal of congenital disease in the population and a wide variety of it. Intermarriage between cousins is popular; it's the preferred form of marriage, so that hereditary disease is encouraged.

The work with adults is mainly with chronically ill patients, quite a few of whom have some kind of equipment at home that they're using. There's dialysis and insulin for diabetics. The Bedouin are in a transition from being nomads to becoming part of an industrial and agricultural society. Infant mortality *is* going down, I think because of the creation of the State: now there's some sort of medical service. Family size is going up all the time.

Dialysis in a tent works fine – it's very interesting to see how people find their own ways to use the resources they have. We've one patient who has a beautifully carved old cane: he hangs the cane and the dialysis bag on one of the poles of the tent and creates a perfect gravitational system.

In this society women have a very separate place from men; a very defined role. A few of them are now at least starting to work, mainly in agriculture and industry like the men. There is fear that if they do leave the home in this way it will become difficult to control them, but as the society is in transition, that's also changing a bit . . . the younger men are a bit more liberal and less frightened of the new situation.

On the other hand, the situation in which the Bedouin are now so often living – without sheep – has in some ways limited the role of women. Someone who used to take the sheep to the fields had some freedom of movement, better than sitting at home all day . . . I think that in name and custom men are certainly in control, but there's some power sharing, more than the stereotype would have it; it depends on the individual family. Women are powerful in maternal care, more than anything else.

The Negev is huge – we could do with a hundred vans rather than just this one. We do encourage those who have the resources to come to Beersheva for their medication, to try and diminish our responsibility a little. We're not designed to do any major work in the field – all I can do is some blood testing, some urine testing.

Then she spent half an hour with Hatma, aged just 14, who had been left at home to care for nine children while her mother was away in hospital. The baby, only 45 days old, was crying miserably, and Varda and Sayyid explained, very carefully, that the child needed feeding every three hours rather than four. Hatma's hands shook with tension as she learnt to measure the required 60 grams of the smaller feed. But when during the new 24 hour cycle would she get any rest herself? The older relatives who lived nearby were concerned and involved, and a small group clustered round the kitchen door as the explanations continued, but they seemed an uncertain support. Hatma, in spite of her youth, is immersed in this new world and the high standards called for by doctors, nurses, hygienists and teachers. It is very like the situation Miriam had to handle after the mass emigration from Yemen and arrival in Israel. And Hatma, who after all is still learning to read, is understandably worried about getting the formula for the baby right.

We had been visiting members of the Abublal tribe that morning: on the same day, several families of the Zanun clan of the Azazma Bedouin were evacuated from the nature reserve at Avdat, and brought to Segev Shalom near Beersheva. The *Jerusalem Post* called the removal peaceful but it came at the end of a five-year struggle by the clan and their leader, Awad Zanun, against being moved. Bedouin men may rule in their homes, but they too lack control of their destiny.

CHAPTER 6

WORK AND NEED

I get up from my bed at five o'clock because the bus comes to take us at half past. It is very old, the bus – it makes a lot of noise and smells all the time of diesel oil. Sometimes it stops. Then we have to climb out and wait for the man to try and fix it, standing in the road. Often it is very dusty. We can laugh when it happens but it is not so very funny – we lose the money if we are too late to the factory.

I work with oranges. Really, it is not very nice in there – quite dark and very wet. We do wear special clothes but often my feet are wet for the whole day. The driver stays there to watch us, although sometimes he does fall asleep! My father say I cannot go to work in the factory if I do not stay with the others from the bus and the village. The man – we call him the Rayis – he is there to watch us for my mother and my father. But that is all right. We are all friends, and we do have some good times – I have been working in the factory nearly two years.

Also I have a little money now to spend, not like before, because my father, he take only half. I can buy a new dress, and also I like to help my mother with new things, and my little sister. Yes, it is alright, but I do get tired. But I am lucky to have the work – here in Nablus there is nothing to do if you are not a teacher or a secretary. Now there are also a few hairdressers, and some women make sweet biscuits.

I went to school for six years but we did not have any books. Yes, I can read and write; some of my friends, they cannot.

That was Jamila, who is 19. She is one of the thousands of workers from the West Bank who cross the Green Line every day to earn their living in Israel, although she earns a lot less than her Israeli counterparts. In addition, women usually earn only two-thirds of the going rate for men. As a legal employee, she pays a National Insurance stamp, but if she loses the job she has paid the stamp for nothing. If she were an Arab employee living within Israel, she *would* get her unemployment benefit, and if she were a member of the Histadrut and one of its unions, that would bring medical benefits as well. Workers from Gaza and the West Bank pay but have no benefits, nor are all the 50,000 men and women who travel into Israel even as fortunate as Jamila: many return to their own beds only once a week and squat illegally 'somewhere in Israel' until their day off. They also squat in police cells when arrested, but the practice remains widespread, for the convenience of employer and to save fares for the employee. The accommodation is sparse and makeshift, often quite squalid.

One of those eager to see rights and benefits extended to all who work in Israel, wherever they may come from, is Amira Andrianov. Now 42, she is the general secretary of the Textile, Garment and Leather Workers Union, the second largest union within the federal structure of the Histadrut, the powerful labour organisation that owns and runs its own industries at the same time as representing the interests of its members in employment throughout Israel. Amira is the only woman in the country to hold such a powerful position.

We have always had a high percentage of women in the textile industry – half our 74,000 members are women. The men have specialised in leather work and the women in textiles, but we are starting to see some men at the sewing machines now – that's very encouraging! Gender roles are so strong . . .

I don't think I got this job because I am a woman. It never even struck me, that, as a woman, it was something special to get this position. Maybe it was because of my childhood, the way I was brought up. It never occurred to me that it might be special to get a job like this; it's only now that I realise how important it is that women should have more of the jobs that are going. At the time I didn't think about it: I thought I was lucky enough to be the best person for the job.

It's a very difficult time for the textile industry right around the world at the moment, but here it's coupled with the Israeli ever-continuing economic crisis; we suffer even more. There's huge competition in textiles between the third world and the so-called advanced part for textile orders – our members have never earned well, and now it's become much worse: a lot of women are being laid off. At best women earn only 150 dollars a month in a textile factory; and they spend nearly half of that on day care for their children: they end up with very little.

We have women from every section working in the garment industry: Arabs, Jews, Muslim, Christian – they all work together under the same conditions – something that's still quite unusual in Israel, where work is often organised on racial and religious lines. They are all members of the union.

In Israel everyone joins the Histadrut first, and then automatically you become a member of the particular union that looks after your own industry. Of course there are still thousands who are unorganised. It happens especially in little villages, but sometimes also in towns . . . the bosses say to employees 'We'll give you better conditions if you don't join the union' – like working the hours they want to work – but then they're also free to fire them when the bosses want!

Workers are not always aware of the disadvantages of being unorganised; sometimes they only come to us when the situation is already tragic; I think you have that happening all over the world; it's not an Israeli problem especially. The other tragic thing that happens here are the jobs, in bad conditions, that Arabs will take. When people need a job badly enough they compromise a lot . . . in England, in France, in Belgium: there are workers who will not take what they think are 'dirt' jobs, the casual jobs that are outside the system. But those who are desperate for work, like a Yugoslav in Germany or an Arab here, take those jobs, and those who refuse – Arab or Jew, as long as they live in Israel and not Gaza or the West Bank – take unemployment benefit instead.

The whole thing is very bad for the working class, for all working people; only the manufacturers do well out of it. Contracts, holidays, pensions – our members do have those, even though their wages are so low. The workers coming in from Gaza and the West Bank don't have those rights, but we are starting to organise them. The building workers have also done a lot for new Arab members from outside Israel: we will get them their rights . . . the building workers are starting to demand the same conditions for all, and there have been some strikes over it.

In the garment industry we have been organising Arab workers from outside for some time: today you will see a lot of people from the occupied territories that are members of the union and, indeed, very active, like shop stewards. We have fought long years over this. As a matter of fact, I started that campaign when I was still a shop steward and when the first Arabs came to work with us.

I can have my person political opinion, like everyone else, but the moment I represent workers I represent them all. I don't care where they live, I don't care about their colour or anything else. My Arab members voted for me – we have a lot of Arab members, more than any other union. We are the second biggest union of all the industries, after the metal workers.

I started on the factory floor at Polgat, the biggest textile factory in Israel, in Kiryat Gat – a development town. I became a shop steward very unwillingly. When I started working at the factory I had planned a career in the job, not in the trade union. So when I was asked, I said I'd be a shop steward for two years – and here I am! Now I'm really married to it, because I was a shop steward for nine years and I've done this job for five . . . at my age it has really become my whole life.

(There is another factory at Kiryat Gat, Iskoor, that is one of the many in Israel that belongs to the Histadrut. Iskoor does not employ any Arab workers and its director, Itzhak Ran, says this policy is pursued to prevent arguments between Arab and Jew. Workers at Iskoor say that unemployment in Israel is high and 'we need jobs for Jews.' The President of Israel, Chaim Herzog, has visited the factory. Amira Andrianov and the textile workers clearly do not have support for their policies among all their fellow members in the Histadrut.)

Amira's mother fought in the Jewish resistance against the British Mandate.

> She would have made a wonderful hippie – she was really against the Establishment. Maybe because my parents were divorced – I lived with my mother – it never occurred to me that being a woman should be something that could stop me in any way. The most respect I've ever had for anyone was for my mother and my aunt: both very strong women. They were more than self-confident: sometimes even our Prime Minister then, Ben-Gurion, couldn't have a discussion with my mother. She really knew what she wanted and she fought for it: I sometimes wondered whether he was afraid of her!
>
> I remember I was very bad at sewing in the primary school, and she made a fight at school that I should be released from the sewing class because I couldn't do anything if I had no gift for it. Eventually they let me do an extra mathematics class instead, but the teacher told me I would have problems later, if I couldn't afford a dressmaker to help me! I believe that my confidence comes from the education I received; and my mother never thought that because one was a woman one should not do this or that . . .

As a leading member of the Histadrut, Amira Andrianov works among the most powerful men and women in Israel: no government can rule without their support and they hold a central position in the formulation of economic policy and the upholding of trade union and welfare rights. During the economic crisis of 1985, for example, when a coalition government achieved a cut in inflation from 445 per cent to 14 per cent in just six months, they were in almost daily consultation with the Histadrut; at one point a general strike was averted only by government concessions to the labour federation.

It is possible that Amira Andrianov's description of the way this mighty federal trade union functions is slightly ingenuous. Other commentators have said that the power exercised by being both trade union and employer has meant that the chief organiser of the workers is also the greatest advocate of keeping wages low; and that the federation is one of the main instruments for policing workers and crushing strikes.

Professor Alice Shalvi, the headmistress of an all girls' school, feels that the inequalities of women at work in Israel are largely determined by religion and the country's continuous state of preparedness for war.

The whole Jewish tradition, Jewish thought as well as Halacha, determines the position of women. There is a clear division of functions and roles, spheres of influence and activity. The women are expected to be active in the household, within the family, and more or less debarred from public action such as actually taking a role in prayer rather than being passive participants. Bearing witness in a court of law — a religious court — is not allowed; our women judges are not allowed to sit in the family courts either, because of their link with religion. The exemption of women from certain duties is based on the central concept that women — for reasons of modesty — should be inside the home and not outside. What began as an exemption gradually became a hard and fast prohibition. (In 1946 an Israeli newspaper, Hatzofe, said of Golda Meir 'It is difficult to see a woman leading a political body in this nation, the nation that coined the phrase "A king's daughter belongs at home".'[1])

Of course women are central in the home in the role of mother, the role of wife: the whole notion of Eshit Shayril.[2]

1 Golda Meir, Israeli Prime Minister 1969–74, was immediately elevated to the role of 'national grandmother'. One of her special virtues was seen to be the motherly instinct that led her to make tea and cakes for the soldiers guarding her house, and to see every Israeli soldier as her son.

2 Eshit Shayril   Proverbs 31. A domestic prayer in praise of a good woman that is used at the Friday evening Sabbath meal.

(A woman of worth, who can find her/for she is more
precious than rubies . . . She looks after her home with
care/and does not idle away her time . . . Charm deceives and
beauty fades/So praise the woman who honours God.) It goes
completely counter to modern conceptions of no
discrimination between the two sexes in activity in the public
domain.

As well as the Jewish tradition there's the whole body of
law in the Halacha, which works most of the time in favour
of the man – as when there's a divorce. Halacha gives
concrete legal expression to the division of roles: that then
expresses itself in status. But Halacha has had no effect on
the 35 per cent of all women who go out to work. That fits
into the very opposite – modern egalitarian thought, and the
legislation passed by the Knesset in the last 38 years. There
we have legislated consistently towards greater equality:
opportunity; rewards; equal pay for equal work. The Knesset
and Halacha really contradict each other.

But there's a third factor in public opinion. What people
think is seen as right. Ironically, popular opinion goes far
more in line with the traditional than with egalitarian
legislation. In fact, even some progressive legislation has
reinforced the notion of women's major function being in the
home. It's only women who can take maternity leave . . . it's
only women who are allowed time off as *their* sick leave
when the child is ill; and working mothers are allowed to
work an hour less than men. All this legislation, which at
first sight seems so beneficial, has the underlying conception
that only women do the parenting.

We women are then left in a trap. You have to make up
your mind to give up preferential legislation and say No: we
want to be completely equal . . . In Scandinavia, mother and
father share the maternity leave: that's what you have to
start going for, that sort of legislation. It really is ironic that
so much of the new legislation, which was intended to help
us go out to work, has boomeranged in this way: instead of
protecting, it ensures that we remain at the bottom of the
pile. Women take part-time work, they resort to all sorts of

strategies in order to combine motherhood and the family with work – flexitime, taking work home, minding other people's children, which they can do while minding their own. And if they drop out of the workforce while their children are young it's very difficult to come back afterwards. Re-entry has not been developed here at all.

Even on the kibbutzim, which talk so much more about equality, the men still go away to the Army; anyway, the women have more or less elected to be the child-minders. It's so much more convenient, if you're nursing your baby, to be with the baby anyway three or four times during the day . . . that's a short period, I know, but it isn't easy to go in and out of the workforce.

You can't keep on swopping about. Very few people have only one child, and it takes years off their time at work. It's connected with the lack of re-entry facilities. It isn't easy for a woman whose taken time off, say six or eight years off, to come back after that and catch up – I'm talking now about professions. Our retraining hardly exists: there's very little encouragement for older women to go back into, for example, the teaching profession, where they could actually do a great deal after they've raised their children.

Too old at 40 is more or less the attitude. I had the case only this week of a woman who is 44, just finished her doctorate in literature, and after all, since retirement age at the University is 68 she has another 24 years to go, to contribute. One would have thought that's not exactly a negligible period, 24 years. And yet she was told by one person after another, head of department, Dean, and so on – You're too old, you can't start – you can have a temporary job only. Women are not on the agenda anywhere . . . the Israeli Press doesn't take women's issues seriously: women's issues go on the women's page, that's all, with the recipes and the fashions, and beauty, and not the political aspects of women's lives.

I think one of the major needs in Israel is to do a great deal of consciousness raising among women; we're not even on the agenda among most *women*. There are all too few women who feel it's important to take up women's issues. There is some waking up to the way women are discriminated against, but it's more a sort of vague uneasiness, a sense that not everything is as it should be. That's partly because there isn't a strong women's movement, not politically. I use every opportunity – what our lobby[3] is doing now is responding to everything in the Press. Even a statement which is not made deliberately discriminatory; people simply using sexist terminology quite unconsciously. Often drawing their attention to it is enough: Oh, oh, you're quite right, I didn't mean that . . .

This was the only home I visited in Israel or the West Bank where a man was cooking the main meal of the day – in this case Professor Shalvi's husband.

Alisa Tamir is one of the Histadrut executive. She worked as a nurse for fifteen years, but even as a student was active in union affairs. She was first nominated to be a Histadrut representative by her political party, Avdut Avodat (Workers Party), but as a nurse. That brought the first realisation that the difficulties faced by women were not confined to the special situation within the health service.

The greatest problem is that women are paid so little; that's linked with the question of equality at work.[4] It's a matter of a stereotype, of an image, because in our society women are widely seen as the 'second' breadwinner in the family. So many women accept this image of themselves. . . . They get the same education as their peers, the men, but they think they haven't got to put in a great deal of effort: they are not the significant breadwinner.

Of course equality is not only about demonstrating or demanding: equality means you actually have to *do* it! First

3 The women's movement lobby among Jewish women is largely middle class. It is small and quite unpopular, even the word 'feminist' evoking hostility. It aims at status for women as much as more general power. Among Arab women the same work is linked with political aspirations for national liberation.
4 Women earn only 14 per cent of total family income.

in education; and then you have to be involved in every part of life and work. You have to put a lot of effort into training and getting a job. A lot of girls still think 'Okay – I'll get myself a man who's doing well, and I'll get my status that way.' Ugh! that's still a problem. Twenty, thirty years ago it was even worse, although sixty years ago, in the beginning of the new Israel when the Histadrut was created, women had a new and revolutionary attitude towards their place in society. They were chalutzot, pioneers, and as everyone knows, they fought and they struggled.

But after a few years they went again into 'their' place – the kitchen, the children, the family. And even today the work they do is in the same tradition: teachers, nurses, social workers. It's a concentrate of the stereotype jobs, the women jobs; and the stereotype suffers from low pay.

When a man in a factory or an office does the same work as the woman next to him, they do earn the same; that's not a problem. The real issue is how the job is evaluated. I have just received the data from a meeting I was participating in, a meeting of our pension fund. Two-thirds of the fund's members are women – but the money they put in, which is linked to their earnings, makes up only 35 per cent of the fund. The men are half their number but they put in double the amount . . . we really have to re-evaluate jobs. Who says a teacher's work is less valuable than an architect's? Or a manager?

The hierarchy affects pay structures as well. The manager, the headmaster, is far more likely to be a man. Even in the teachers' trade union, with its overwhelming number of women members, the high positions are held by men. That neat picture in our pension fund – two-thirds of the members: women. And two-thirds of the earnings: men. What a paradox! And the trustees are all men except for two women. Our society is controlled by men. They are our government, our Parliament, our trade union leaders, and all their thinking and their attitudes suit men and *their* lives.

Here in the Histadrut I have a lot of arguments and a lot of problems to convince my colleagues that we are exactly like men. We need the same job, the same salary; we are the breadwinners like our husbands. They won't accept it from me! Unemployment is growing and thousands of people are losing their jobs – and most of them are women. Of course, they say, she is not the breadwinner. They see her earnings as pocket money, a little less for dresses; but if we fire him, they make a great fuss. We are working to change that view, but it's not a one-day business, like a strike or a revolution. Not all the women support us: we have to re-educate them, too.

She is working, she is cooking, she is typing, she has to take care of the children – everything in one minute! The stress that a woman is in – it's not fair, and we are working to make things a little bit easier, to change her life. And if women are the lower paid, Arab women have it even worse. They do not have the education of the Jewish women; most of them are girls from the country. Even if they have education the family are often not agreed that they should work. They cannot compete for jobs, they have to stay very very near their home, their mother, their father. All the factories that are in their villages are factories of textiles, of low paid workers, and they are exploited. The concentration of Arab women in these jobs is very high, much more than the Jewish women, but they do all get the same salaries . . . we are the Histadrut of everybody: we have here Arab colleagues, both in Israel and the West Bank.

The executive committee has Arab members. Here, in my department, we are about to take on an Arab woman to help organise the Arab women workers. We have to find somebody who is independent from her family, to be allowed to move from place to place and stay away from home. She needs a car, to go from one village to another.

We are so occupied with the double burden we have, with the family and the job – and then war, that women are not willing to be very active in the third job. This is the representation, this is policital power, to be very active in political parties – you need much more time for that. And the men of course are not so enthusiastic to share in domestic work. We need to raise their consciousness . . . we hold a lot of seminars for workers and for shop stewards: they sit there for three days, in locations all over Israel. We are not militant enough in the political parties – I am a member of the Labour Party: even there. Twenty-five Labour members in the coalition government, and not one woman. A hundred and twenty members of the Knesset, and only ten women . . . yet in the Labour Party we are 50 per cent of all members.

It's true that the workers from Gaza and the West Bank have lower wages, less job security and, usually, no union membership. I'm very sorry that this is the situation – we have not coped with this; and of course 90 per cent of those low-paid workers are women, whether Arab or Jew. Arab men do worse than Jewish men.

The Histadrut really has a unique role in affecting government policies – it is a very powerful organisation, with 80 percent of the Israeli population being members – not just those with work. It's not only a trade union; it also handles health insurance, the pension – all sorts of welfare, including that of the women's organisation, Na'amat. In Israel, if you're unemployed, you're still a member of the Histadrut; if you're married to a worker, you're a member. The trade union section in which I work is only one of nine departments here. And everyone votes within their own section. So we do hold power, but as women we do not use it enough.

Netiva Ben Yehuda worked for the Ministry of Labour before turning to writing as a full-time career. She feels that the desire for equality by women means participating in the 'equality' of stress: if women accept that they also have to accept the competitiveness that is integral to men's working lives in Israel if they are Jewish.

I worked for the Ministry of Labour for a long time – sixteen years. We tried very hard to push women forward but we didn't manage it. I think that women themselves don't want to climb up – that's not a phenomenon only in Israel, it's all over the world. You *can* succeed like Margaret Thatcher or

Golda Meir did, but you don't have to: women can also become part of the elite without working quite so hard, without getting heart attacks or ulcers in your stomach.

You can use your education and get to a comfortable place and then sit there . . . once they made an investigation about all the people in government in Israel: a high percentage work for the government and they looked at how long a person stays in one post, in the same rank. Twenty percent moved on after three years, 30 after four years, 10 after five years – and me, I was the only one, after twelve years. I was in the same rank for twelve years but I didn't bother; and all the others staying in the same place for a long time were women. People said to me 'Imagine, if a man is in the same job for more than three years, his wife, his neighbours, his mother – everyone ask him "Are they all better than you"' – so he gets up and fights his way to the top. I didn't have this ridicule, so I stayed. Why not? Why not stay the same way – I had enough money and it's raised automatically every year: I didn't want for anything. So no one laughed, and I just stayed peacefully: I was not less accepted. It's the same in the law – at University half the students are women but there are only two women judges. In the Army too – eight women officers for every 400 men. I've told my daughter since her childhood that we women are so lucky . . . this generation can choose to have a career or we can stay at home and nobody laughs at us.

Carmit Gie also sees the road to equality as strewn with all sorts of unexpected boulders:

On the face of it, women are equal in Israel: but they're not really so. What the men do is give us an opportunity to be like them, to be men, plus being mothers and housewives and so on; so we have to be superwomen. The greatest tragedy is that they won't come into the 'womanly' aspects of childcare and domestic work: they assume a toughness and they ignore feelings and emotions. They're not allowed to cry: the greatest thing you can say about someone is: 'He didn't cry at his son's funeral.' This is the supreme thing you could say about a man. In the same way, they don't spend very much time with their children, because it's not done. I pity them. . . .

I think they also want women to put them on a pedestal. I think because they ignore the so-called feminine aspects of their own personality, they expect it to be fulfilled by their women. If they are not weak, if they are not emotional, then they are men. But that's not a human thing to be, so they need all the encouragement from their women. They want you to look after them, love them, cherish them, and put them on a pedestal.

Who wants freedom from a family for the sake of a career? It's the old question that's never asked of men. In Israel it remains topical – Golda Meir felt it was a choice she had to make (her marriage broke up as she became prominent in Israeli political affairs), and one she regretted very much. My feeling was that women accepted and wanted their childminder role and set their work sights lower as a consequence. It was a bit like Netiva Ben Yehuda's climbing – so happily – out of the rat race in her male-dominated government department, saying that as a woman she didn't need all that stress and hassle for the sake of kudos and some extra shekels.

Jewish women don't want the competition, they demand shorter hours (there's the other problem that an early schoolday means a long, free afternoon for the children), and a preponderance of them told me they didn't want too much responsibility outside the home: there was enough to do already! These constraints, coupled with the powerful social ethic that surrounds the dictates of a military life and the strength of the military tradition, creates a pattern that even those who are not religious cannot ignore. War has not emancipated women, it has given them an even clearer domestic base, and many of them relish it.

My own concern is with the result of such an abdication of power and responsibility, and what it could mean for the attempt to go from war to peace. I don't have any kind of belief that women are better at peace initiatives; but it means that a large chunk of those who are centrally involved in war are missing from the debates and meetings about the most urgent issue in an Israel that burns with hatred and continually incipient military action. Women who are not independent and who lack power over their own lives also lack the even more significant democratic strength to influence the policies of their party and their Government. They need work, but they need parity in the assembly even more than the market-place.

CHAPTER 7

THREE PIONEERS

In a land riven by bitter political and religious differences, Ora Namir, Samicha Khalil and Chaike Grossman share a great passion – the love of the common piece of territory they all live in. Chaike Grossman grew up in Poland, yet she knew intimately the outlines of the holy land to which she was to come after the second world war. Samicha Khalil and Ora Namir were born scarcely twelve miles apart – Mrs Khalil in Tayibeh, near Netanya, where her father was the headmaster of the local school, and Mrs Namir in what was then only a settlement but is today the town of Haderah. She comes from working-class origins. But only two of these three fine pioneers of Israel and Palestine have ever met: the trio have never been able to discuss their mutual love, nor their profound belief that all human beings have the right to dignity and political participation in the society based on that land.

The laws of Israel as well as mutual suspicion and caution have helped prevent such a meeting. Although Mrs Khalil, who has lived on the West Bank since 1948, has never been charged with breaking any law or military regulation, she is clearly regarded as a danger to the status quo: she has been served with numerous town arrest orders and been consistently denied the opportunity to travel abroad, either to visit her children and grandchildren or to attend the international conferences to which she has been invited. She believes in an independent Palestine: an aim that smacks of the aspirations of the outlawed Palestine Liberation Organisation. Today, in Israel or beyond, it is illegal for an Israeli citizen to even meet with such a person.

113

Mrs Namir and Mrs Grossman, as members of the Knesset, must see each other regularly although they, too, have their political differences. Both regard themselves as Zionists and socialists, but Mrs Grossman's party – Mapam – has refused to join the coalition with the Right that has enabled the parliamentary system to continue functioning since 1984. Mapam is far more rigorous in its defence of human rights than Ma'arach, the main Labour grouping on whose executive Mrs Namir serves. The Ma'arach coalition with Likud has led to government by rotation.

Mrs Namir, who has chaired a government commission to inquire into matters of equal opportunity and equality for women, is especially concerned with pensions. Mrs Grossman is the Deputy Speaker of the Knesset she has served with such skill and verve for many years. Mrs Khalil is as hardworking, and as dedicated: in 1965 she and a few friends started the Society of In'ash El-Usra near Ramallah to provide vocational training courses for young women. Today 250 come to learn business and secretarial work, embroidery, sewing, knitting, baking and beauty culture. Eighty per cent of the graduates find work, some at home because that is still more acceptable to many Muslim families, but an increasing number away, in a more independent milieu.

That may sound innocuous enough, but Samicha Khalil believes that even such developments for the Arabs of the West Bank are anathema to the military administration. She cites the fact that it took eighteen months to get permission to buy a bus for the society, which now houses the orphan sons and daughters of Arab families, or those who are in prison because of their political beliefs. In fact, while the group works in the most general way for the 'raising of the social, financial, cultural and educational standards of women so that they may become active, responsible and independent members of their community', it makes no secret of the political aspiration for an independent Palestine: there's the rub – it would be quite inappropriate for the three, all politically committed, to come anywhere near each other.

Mrs Namir's work on the commission, which looked at every

9 A fiery talker and an important Israeli author, Netiva Ben Yehuda has fought for popular, 'street' Hebrew to become as acceptable as the biblical variety

10 A Labour Member of Parliament, Ora Namir has spent a lifetime in political and welfare work. Equality, she says, is despised by her male colleagues in the Knesset.

11 Born in Israel (then Palestine), Samicha Khalil fled to the West Bank in 1948. She has been active in the struggle for equal national rights for Arabs ever since.

12 Chaike Grossman was a partisan in Poland. She emigrated to Israel, and today is Deputy Speaker of the Knesset.

13 Hira Schachter is a founder member of Kibbutz Barkai. She feels women are still second-class participants in the life of the kibbutz.

14 Kibbutz Barkai – women at work, but not always in traditional roles.

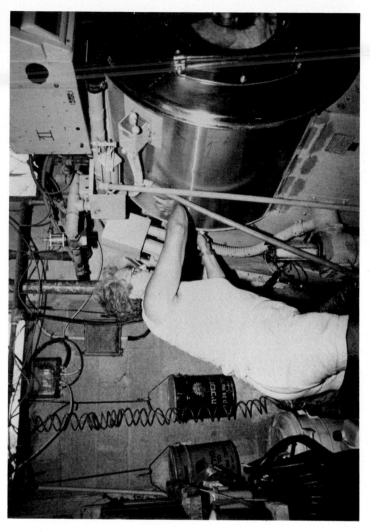

15 From agriculture into industry. The move away from the land has become typical of the kibbutzim.

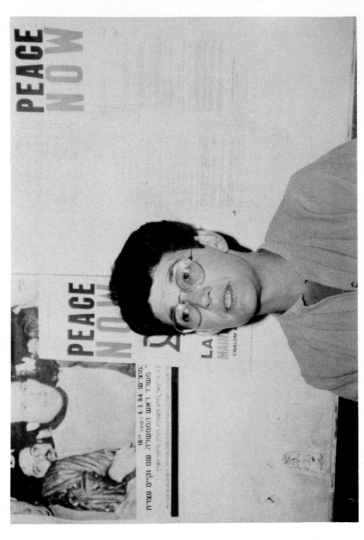

16 Janet Aviad of Peace Now. When a hundred thousand Israelis demonstrate against war, that's like four million Americans taking to the streets . . . .

aspect of the life of women, made her think that:

> The main problem is not more equality between men and women, but much more one of more equality between women and women. We found that half of all Israeli women – and I speak only about the Jewish population, it is much worse among Arab women – have only eight years of schooling. They start school at 5, and, although they should have eleven years of tuition, many have far less. In fact nearly a quarter leave school again barely able to read and write. I think that's the main problem. Why? Because when we look at the better educated women in spite of the fact it is very, very hard for them to combine work outside their home, family and children, they still do it and we know that in most of the families, maybe 98 or 99 per cent of them, women do all the domestic work as well.
>
> The interest that they have in a life of work gives them the strength to combine two working days in one day and we saw, for example, that among men and women who have a bachelor degree, 74 per cent of the men are working and 70 per cent of the women are working. When we go down to the people with lesser educational achievements 70 per cent of the men go to work, but among women not more than 20 per cent.
>
> To my regret we did not have enough representation, enough statistics or sufficient material to look into the real situation of Arab women. We had a few Arabs on the committee – both men and women – but that was not sufficient for the necessary background work.
>
> Personally, I think we need another commision. You see, when we had prepared our findings I had to present them to the Prime Minister then, Menachem Begin. I am a member of the Labour Party and we were in opposition to Begin's Likud at the time, so he did nothing. If there had been a Labour administration then our suggestions would have been taken more seriously: I say that even though I am very, very annoyed at the attitude of my fellow men in the Labour Party towards women.

Think of it: we have a government of 25 Ministers and members of the Cabinet, and there isn't a single woman there. They still all believe that as long as we have our woman's organisation in the Histadrut it will be enough. Let the women play women's business. They will not share power with us.

If I take the Knesset as an example: we are not many women, we are ten women here from different parties, and I think that if you compare the women's activities in the Knesset to the men's activities in the Knesset, in each party they are more devoted, they are more sensitive, . . . you will see them more at work in the plenary, in the committees, on tours, touring the country, meeting people far more than the men. So we do the hard work but when it comes to power or representation men and men alone rule. It is not only the question of the religious parties in Israel and their power. Yes, the religious ones are more powerful than their number warrants, but they derive the power from the proportional representation system of election in Israel; because of the coalition, because of the fact that the public has never given any majority either to the Labour, or to the Likud, and when we form a coalition we always have to take them into it. Their price is very high.

In Israel the power of the religious parties in the Knesset and the power of religion over the life of women is linked. If they did not have the strength to keep a government ruling the country, they would not be able to force so much religious law on to women either. I think it's not true only about the Jewish religion. If you go to Italy and you see the power of the Catholic Church, they are very influential. Nowhere does religion and orthodoxy go together with the advancement of women, it just doesn't.

For them a woman is second, for them a woman should stay at home, be almost constantly pregnant, bring children into the world and that's it . . . cook well, clean well, bake well, press well, do laundry well. That goes with their way of thinking.

Ora Namir feels that she herself got into politics by a

coincidence initially, rather than by commitment.

I was married to the Mayor of Tel Aviv and I found it
difficult to accept that, as the wife of the Mayor, I should cut
ribbons and open bazaars. I had always, since I can
remember, had a strong sense of responsibility, of caring for
people and for children. You could call it a strong emotion
for volunteer work. I decided I must do something more
serious, and then I started to be very much involved in youth
clubs, youth centres, mostly in the under-privileged parts of
Tel Aviv. I became very involved as a volunteer in the
working mother's organisation, Na'amat, which runs crèches
as well as vocational education for girls. Then my husband
suddenly became very ill, and I had to find paid work, and I
was pressed to take over the secretaryship of Na'amat. That
led to the Knesset six years later.

Somewhere we have stopped in the advancement of the
status of women: for Jewish women there was some growth,
with more women judges and doctors and lawyers, but even
so at the level of decision-making we have the same number
of women and in many places even less. I can't say that we
have been an influence for Arab women. Maybe in some way
they are a little, a very little more advanced, but I think that
not only in this aspect but in many aspects we paid very little
attention to the Arab population. The main reason is the
conflict, the constant conflict . . . war, Arabs surrounding
us . . . enemies . . . it has been very difficult.

It is very difficult for an Israeli, especially the young Israeli,
to differentiate between an Arab outside our border and an
Arab inside Israel and we have to understand one thing: I do
not believe that one day they will really love us, or we shall
really love them, but we have to find more and more ways to
live well together because our destiny is the same one. The
status of Arab women is just a part of that whole situation.
And because the West Bank is not a part of Israel it means
that the services that exist there for women are far less than
here.

I don't want the West Bank or Gaza to be part of this

country, and they don't want it either. I am very much for giving back the areas that are mostly populated by Arabs, so that there may be peace, and I regret the fact that I do not represent the way of thinking of the majority here.

We have just won a very small victory in the Knesset for Arab families. As a result of the inflation it was decided to cut the welfare benefits for large families, but less for those who had been in the Army. As you know, Arabs do not serve . . . their children would have suffered very much, so we went to the Prime Minister and he acceded to our request to keep the same benefit for all big families.

As far as my own party, the Labour Party, is concerned I feel very uncomfortable and disappointed. Partly it's our own fault because our women members accept that we should concentrate on 'women's affairs'. Education, health, welfare – they don't do a thing for our advancement in political life. When we face a debate in which a woman debates with a man, it's always on those issues. I've come to the conclusion that the men, the important ones that make the decisions, find it very convenient to let the women have their women's organisation, whether Zionist or Histadrut or political. Let us play in our own play yard!

We must change our behaviour in politics, in the academic world, everywhere. We are equal and we will not sit and concentrate only on the social issues. More women should sit on the Finance committee, on the Defence and Foreign Relations committee . . . we must act like the men on politics, on the territories, on foreign relations, not only on day crèches and vocational training for girls, and big families. We really have to change things.

Mrs Namir, who is a leading spokesperson on education in the Knesset, also chairs a governmental pensions committee. On the day of the interview the chief civil servant who implements its work had publicly disagreed with her: she was convinced that he would not have behaved in that way if she had been a man.

The representation of women in the Knesset is low, at

6 per cent of the total; among local councils it is even worse – only 4.6. In many areas the religious groups combine to keep out women candidates, but no one has so far fought that issue in the courts.

Although Samicha Khalil was born so near Ora Namir's birthplace in the Palestine of the British Mandate, she has lived near Ramallah on the West Bank since her family fled there in 1948. She has never been charged with breaking any law or military regulation. Yet, where Mrs Namir has gradually moved closer to the centre of political power in Israel, Mrs Khalil holds no power at all, and is not even allowed to travel – either back into Israel when she wanted to bury her husband on the family plot at Netania, or to Jordan to visit her children. Here is her story.

The facts of my life are simple. I am over 60 and have lived in this area for many years.

I am a mother who has brought up five children, in the sometimes difficult conditions of war and dislocation. Two of my five children have been deported from the West Bank and are not allowed to return to visit me. All five children live abroad. I am a widow and I now live alone in El Bireh. Because my children live abroad, I have often wished to travel to see them. I have made repeated efforts, but since 1980, I was allowed to travel to Jordan only once, for a week in 1983.

I hope it is not the aim of the military authorities to block the normal wish of a mother to see her children. So I continue to ask why; why am I denied permission to travel? I turn to my life as a professional woman – does the reason lie there? For the past twenty years, I have been the head of a women's charitable society, In'ash El-Usra, which is located in the town of El Bireh, where I reside. Our society has developed from a few women volunteers to an organisation that employs 86 people and supports 3000 families. Our society performs a wide range of services for women and children in our community: we hold classes to teach women employable skills; we maintain a daycare centre; we have productive activities to employ people and to raise money for our society; we publish a folklore magazine and maintain a museum of Palestinian craft and dress. We give scholarships to needy students and we support families who have no breadwinner. Do any of these activities constitute a reason to deny me permission to travel? I would think not.

To be sure, I, like most heads of charitable societies in the West Bank, have been questioned about my activities by the military authorities. At times, they have expresed disapproval of the aid we have given to prisoners' children, for example. But our mission is the welfare of *all* children; we do not deny bread or milk to any hungry child. Surely this cannot be a reason to deny me permission to travel?

Yet I have consistently been denied permission to leave the West Bank, either to see my children or to attend international conferences on issues that concern my work here, such as the welfare of Palestinian families or the preservation of Palestinian culture. Indeed, for a full two and a half years, from 1980 to 1982, I could not even 'travel' beyond the municipal boundaries of the town of El Bireh. In those years, the authorities imposed five successive town-arrest orders upon me – for periods of six months each. The military authorities even called me from the deathbed of my husband, despite my pleas, to read me one of the town arrest orders. Again, these orders are issued without any specific charge or reason and there is no opportunity to challenge the order in a court of law.

Even after the town-arrest orders expired, I was still not allowed to travel. In late 1983, I issued an Open Appeal to All Mothers. In this appeal, I said: 'Since denial of permits to visit is not subject to condition or time limits, this effectively means that years may pass without the possibility that I would see my children. This denial of the right of a mother to see her children is contradictory with the most basic international human and legal rights.'

I believe this reaches the heart of the matter. I am in the inhuman situation of enduring a denial of my freedom from a power that is not accountable in any way. This authority will not give me any reason for this denial, nor to provide me with means to defend my case or to challenge the denial.

Why did we start a girls' school? For thousands of years women worked only in the fields, caring for animals, and at home. But during the British Mandate women did more than planting, harvesting and looking after the chickens: they fought and demonstrated for the first time.

We lost our lands as a result of the British occupation; we have never been free to create education everywhere. I'd like to create literacy centres in many places, but I'm denied the chance.

We've been stopped from living our own lives since 1917: if we had our own independent State we could choose our education; and we could make our own health system. I believe that emancipation of our women and our freedom will go hand in hand. To be elected to Parliament; to be a president; to be a mayor – who shall we ask for that right? First we want our political freedom . . . any peoples under an occupation have to attend to two major problems – the question of bread and that of the occupation itself. We cannot even do a great deal about the low wages – and women earn even less than the men – while we are under the occupation.

Do you know that most of the Arabs who go to work in Jerusalem or in Israel get no sick leave, no holidays and no medical help? And that many of them are made to pay the Israeli national insurance stamp, but they still don't see any of the money coming back? What is right or fair about that? They need the bread . . . At the same time the military won't let us develop our own factories and our business here. They stopped us building the cement factory, because the one in Israel sells cement here . . . it took us a year and a half just to buy a bus for the children! A year and a half; we even had to get a lawyer to help us get the permissions! That is occupation for you. Did you know that 80 per cent of the goods here on the West Bank come from Israel?

To get our own goods out of the West Bank is sometimes impossible for us . . . you know we make embroidery here, the traditional embroidery? We wanted to sell it in Amman, so we went to cross at the Allenby Bridge – four times we had to go to Allenby: they held the embroidery there for seven months, and water got into the cloth suitcases. Then they charged us a thousand dollars. I believe they did it on purpose to try and stop our small project. Can you believe it? Such a small project. . . .

When my husband died, I asked permission to take his body to bury it in Tayibeh, where he grew up and where we lived until 1948 near Netanya. We had to keep his body in a fridge for three days, while the arguments went: then the Governor rang up to say it was not possible. So we buried him here – it is also Palestinian land, here in El Bireh. But there we had our house, our fields, our memories . . . here we are all together like insects in a bottle. We want to live on our own land.

You know, we have fourteen kindergartens here, and when we ask the children to make drawings it is always of war: they have killed our love. The children want guns to shoot the Jews . . .

When Chaike Grossman was 19 she became a leader of the underground, among the resisters in the ghettos of Poland who lived under Nazi rule and the daily realities of deportation and extermination, from 1941 to 1945. Then, in 1948, she arrived in Israel:

I was so weak in the first days, in May '48. I came with the first ship, which went to Haifa as a Jewish port. I was coming from war and bombs to more war, more bombs, but I had the feeling I came home. I felt it would be good. I knew Hebrew – it was my first or second language: no one would believe I was a newcomer.

During the second world war, because she did not look Jewish, she had spent a great deal of time on Nazi trains, travelling from one ghetto to another in the attempt to keep them informed and mount a uniform resistance; she had also found local peasants from whom to buy guns. When she arrived in Haifa her first question was 'Tell me please, you have guns? You have enough guns?' Yet today Chaike Grossman wants peace, peace above everything: peace with the Arabs outside Israel and equality for those who live on the West Bank and Gaza. When people say to her 'How can you believe in humanity, after what you saw? How can you believe in peace, and peace with the Arabs?' she replies that it is precisely because of her witness of terminal horror, genocide and human atrocity in Poland that she knows, above all else, that Jews have to approach other peoples with full humanity and democracy. In her work as a member of the Knesset (and as a Deputy Speaker of the Parliament) she is a dove: she argues potently against all those who seek to use the Jewish experience of the holocaust to say that no non-Jew can be trusted – or, of prime importance in Israel, given equal opportunities and rights.

In 1948 she came to a Palestine that had a familiar geography, and Israel, as a well-known ideal, could readily be superimposed. She could easily establish contact with others and arrived as a member of the socialist youth movement, Hashomer Hatzair. But paradoxically, some things weren't right, even then.

From the first step, and before the establishment of the
State – Israel was too narrow for me: not provincial, but not
open-minded enough. Even the leadership of my own party
(Mapam); I clashed with them because they saw Jewishness
only from the view of Israel . . . I couldn't accept it; it is
broader both within Jewish life and in its universal meaning.
My political differences are connected with my
biography – the worst people here in Israel lump all non-
Jews together, as though they were Nazis . . . I had to live
among Nazis and I know that to be a terrible and dangerous
generalisation, and a false one.

[Much of prophetic Judaism had taught the principles of ethics, justice and mercy in contrast to the alluring temptation to imitate other nations and crave for might and power – the concept of Zion meant to live according to the word of the

Lord, and the yearning for the land of Zion was seen as a metaphor for a spiritual passion. Ed.]

Mrs Grossman became a Member of the Knesset in 1968. She has always been interested in women's rights.

> You know, we have some problems and Israel is a very complicated State; we have all kinds of progress from one side and regression from the other. As well as movement on rights for women, we also have the Halacha – and it exists in law, this ancient and religious set of rules. If you are born, and if you die, you have to do with the Halacha. If you are Jewish, you have to marry according to its customs – you have to enter the ritual bath the day before the wedding. We do have two Jewish women judges, but they are not allowed to sit in the family courts because the rabbis have a stranglehold there. Again – we made a law that a company can't get money from the government if it doesn't have equal opportunity policies for men and women; but it's difficult to implement because women are so slow to apply for promotion.

Her ideals of equality between men and women, Arab and Jew are words on thin paper fluttering away in the hot wind, the khamsin, that is Israel's reality today. She accepts residential segregation of Jew and Arab in towns and settlements because, she believes, cultural identity is at stake – 'The Arabs want to live together; they have no reason to live in Jewish towns.' At the same time she and her party, Mapam, have supported the demonstrations over the years of those who, like the Arab villagers of Birim in Galilee, were expelled in 1948, their places taken by Jewish settlers. (In this support she and Mrs Namir do not agree and it would be possible to establish common ground with Samicha Khalil.) But Mrs Grossman also supports the Jewish National Fund, Keren Hayesod, which since 1901 has acquired 85 per cent of Israeli land and holds it in perpetuity, as well as the law of tehannem which forbids the selling or giving of land to any non-Jew. How does she explain the contradiction?

I have only one life: it's based on a combination of Zionism and humanity, Zionism and socialism. I cannot be one without the other; it would be only half a life. That was what brought me to the work in the ghetto – the feeling that Zionism could solve our problems, and the belief that it had to be done in a socialist and humanitarian way.

She went on to speak about her life:

When I worked in the underground in Poland I was continually afraid. If someone says they weren't afraid, they lie. From June 1941, when the Nazis came, I was in and out of the ghetto all the time. My face did not look Jewish; I could travel by train . . . but I was in a state of tension twenty-four hours a day. I also had to deal with the Polish peasants, because they had the guns. It was not simple – and I was still very young: everyone said I looked 16, but I was 20. Of course I had documents saying I was Polish . . . all the time, in spite of the tension, I think I was also happy, because there wasn't a single moment that I wasn't being active against the Nazis. I did not sit down and wait for them to come and take me . . . to do something, to be independent, to have the feeling that you are not a victim . . . I was lucky.

When I landed in Haifa in 1948 I knew every place, every name. I came to work on a kibbutz; and I said when I got there – I want to work only in agriculture. But they sent me to the kitchen: I was so unhappy! It was the worst way to approach a woman like me. Eventually they did let me work in the fields, but only for six months. Then I married and wrote the first book about what it had been like to try and defend the ghetto in Bialystok. Then – and it came at the time of the very big immigration of Jews from Morocco, from Iraq, India, North Africa – I was asked to be the mayor in Western Galilee. We called it the Mabarot, that immigration. I did the job for two years in terrible circumstances: we had 25,000 people, living in dreadful conditions.

The new immigrants came to me, they demonstrated. We want work, we want bread – they really had nothing. I went to see Golda Meir – she was the Minister of Labour then – and told her something, some work had to be found for the people to do. We managed it, to give them bread and butter. You know, so many people came to Israel after the War of Independence, in such a short time. They were mostly refugees, from the world war, from the Arab countries. I was the mayor of a very big area . . . it was dreadful, very hard.

In 1968 Chaike Grossman was elected to the Knesset: like Golda Meir, she has spent her life enmeshed in Israeli politics. As a woman she has been discriminated against only once, she feels – when she was first sent to work in the kitchen on the kibbutz near Naharia in spite of her urgent plea to labour in the fields. As a left-wing socialist, she is among the diminishing minority who believe in equal rights and opportunities for Arabs within Israel, and the return of most of the West Bank to Arab autonomy. She feels she learnt the lessons of a common humanity – diminish one and you diminish all – as she wept at the graves of Bialystok.

Will she and Mrs Namir ever meet Samicha Khalil? Will the three of them be able to share, on a full and equal basis, the land on which all their lives rest so profoundly?

CHAPTER 8

KIBBUTZ BARKAI

Some people in the cities, who haven't visited any kibbutzim,
think that we're rich – that we love to be rich, and that we're
above everybody else. I think, in a way we are. It's not
because we have all the food we can eat, or we have a
swimming pool open all the time. It's because we work
together, we're a large community; we're a group of people
that enjoy each others' company. And we get things together
as a group so that we can use them.

Tamar Livney

Two young Israeli schoolteachers who had been murdered by
Arab shepherds still in their teens were being buried in their
home towns of Afula and Hadera the day I visited Kibbutz
Barkai, mid way between the two in the fertile plain south of
Caesarea. The headlines that morning shouted Anti-Arab
Fever; as a result, hundreds of extra police had been posted,
backed up by the Army. Two days earlier when the bodies –
already badly decomposed – had been discovered in a local
cave after days of searching, the response had been instant
violence: local Arabs had been beaten and stoned, their shops
and cars and petrol stations attacked.

Now, in the midday heat, I wondered idly whether the
Jewish attackers would get three years for stonethrowing
(which was what happened to Arabs on the West Bank) and
whether the homes of the shepherds' parents, which had been

127

bulldozed that morning before ever the young men came to trial – the summary justice that is part of military rule on the West Bank – were actually on the West Bank or within Israel proper, where Arabs do have civil and legal rights. Should I go to Afula? Every Western journalist in Israel would be there among the 20,000 local people, all of them coming to schoolteacher Yosef Eliahu's burial.

Instead, I visited the Arab town of Baqa Al Kirbaya before going the extra five miles to Barkai. I wanted to avoid meandering about in the dark when I returned that evening for the play being put on by the Jerusalem-based drama company El Hakawati. Where was the community centre? An obliging schoolteacher – his pupils bent double, painting white lines down the main road as a vacation task and a communal contribution – detached a 14-year-old from his paintbrush. Said took me to the community centre, told me that Said means Happy and politely said goodbye.

I went on to Barkai and became immersed in kibbutz group dynamics and internal gender politics. At Barkai, right next to the Green Line border so dramatically overthrown in 1967 when the West Bank became Israeli dominated and controlled, the old war bunkers were still visible, now decorated with large, painted flowers. But if war and invasion had receded with new borders, there was still a sense of immediate menace: it resided today in the general fear of Arab terrorism.

All the local lines of communication – and there are other Arab villages in the vicinity, in addition to Baqa – have disappeared during the past few years of tension, except for occasional summer visits to the kibbutz by Arab schoolchildren. Interns for Peace, a seven-year exercise in developing local relationships by joint local activities and mutual help, left not a whiff of permanent friendships when it came to an end two years ago.

The tensions, on that day of the Afula funeral, felt inbred. I planned to drive to an Arab area, by myself, in darkness? The worried looks were polite and anxious. Hira Schachter, lucid, profoundly upset about the growth of a racist right in her country and the growing demand for less democracy rather than more, expressed it for all. She had caught the wrong bus home one day, and found herself in Baqa at half past two one afternoon instead of at Barkai: she had been terrified. How could I possibly go there at night, and by myself? It made me apprehensive when I approached the community centre. Where to find a street light to park under? A wraith detached itself from the shadows – Hullo, hullo: Said had decided to chaperon me to the play.

The Eye and the Tooth was entrancing, a boisterous parable where Arab and Jew fall in love (in reality rather a rare event), have children, shoot each other. Its grotesque figures and visual images of a gross and vulgar materialism were easy to understand even if one didn't speak Arabic, and the message was clear: a kind of harmony *had* existed in the past but now the land is in a permanent state of civil war. In the auditorium the – mainly young – audience voiced warm approval. I sat next to a young woman of 16 with a long, fat pigtail and glowing eyes. Haifa was eager to practise her English, and she invited me back to her home after the play.

She leads a comfortable and sheltered life in the sprawling town, which was in one of the most prosperous Arab areas I saw anywhere in Israel or the West Bank. The high school has books, her parents live well, and she expects to be able to go to University. I'm sure she'll go. Yet as we sat and sipped our strong black coffee she returned again and again, not to her own life as a young Arab woman in Israel, but to the general question of discrimination. What do you think? Haven't we got rights as Palestinians? We want to run our own lives . . . there was no bitterness, no hatred, only a kind of shining ardour. Haifa has her ideals, and they are as strong as any I met in Israel.

I had seen fear in Barkai in the afternoon; that night there was anger and the stale taste of death in Afula. There was no menace in Haifa's brown eyes, only a great dedication. All were linked, and they seemed to have very little to do with the interminable international attempts to get Arab and Jew to sit down together to decide the future of one and a half million people in Gaza and the other occupied territories.

Until 1949 the local Arab landowner Abdul Hadi farmed 13,000 acres in the fertile valleys on either side of his stone mansion on low hills between Hadera and Afula. Today Kibbutz Barkai has turned 8,000 of them into lush green fields of vegetables and feed for cows. There are bananas and avocados, poultry and a plastics factory that accounts for an increasing share of total output. The kibbutz belongs to the Mapam group and does not believe in using – exploiting – the labour of others, either Arab or Jew, to help make a comfortable life for the six hundred people who live in the pleasant, simple accommodation, on green laws and shaded foothills. Over the years, the accumulation of trees and shrubs and the establishment of a swimming pool has made unbearable summers bearable.

Barkai is a delightful place. Internal quiet, no cars, no domestic chores unless one chooses to do a bit of cooking for friends at home – you see all your friends around the dining area anyway – and the most comprehensive support system in the world for bringing up children and creating mature, self-confident, caring adults. Forty years after independence, as the first kibbutzniks who worked so hard to create the cooperative grow older, some of those now middle-aged have volunteered to be trained how to help the elders have a better time in the next years. That those going off to do the courses are all invariably women is an indication of how, in this egalitarian community, traditional roles persist even though there have been times when the positions that hold most power – secretary, for example – have been held by a woman. Yet – as Ionna told me – you might be given, or elected to, a powerful job, as she was in organising the work list, but when men didn't like the arrangements she'd made they just ignored female decisions and went over her head to the next man in line. . . .

Barkai has no delinquency and no formal controls over members. Men, women and children are self-motivated. All are cared for and all contribute; today, with an annual budget of five million (British) pounds, there are no shortages. Holidays, the loan of a car, a paid year off for young men and women when they've done their Army service – it's not, perhaps, surprising that right-wing allegations that kibbutzniks lead an elitist life has found favour in the public eye. But whether that's accurate or not, the tranquillity and caring atmosphere on Barkai has not cut back the rate of heart attacks, nor has it meant that kibbutz members are not stressed by the tensions and fears that Israel's citizens generally feel. Arcadia, it seems, cannot be created in isolation.

The kibbutz plastics factory, when I visited it in the late afternoon, was full of energetic young men ably handling the machinery, with women doing lighter work. The twin assumptions that men must labour so that women can be in labour has informed this kibbutz from the start. (Although why that means that from the moment of conception, or birth, until old age women should only be able to sew, or teach or nurse for ever thereafter has never been rationally explained by the male theorists.) At Barkai the women grumble, but on the whole they accept the stereotyping. Their frustrations are real, but often when they actively begin to rebel they find they've left it too late and a life pattern is set.

Barkai women are pushed or encouraged into those stereotypes in spite of their shorter commitment to total childcare. At six weeks each child enters the nursery, and parents visit and feed as often as they like. Home visits are regular, but the opportunity to take greater responsibility outside is clearly easier. Collective childcare, with its roots in the concept of the kibbutz as one family, has not brought practical results for either women or men in any major restructuring of gender roles. Hira Schachter, a founder member of the kibbutz, gives her reasons why that opportunity was lost.

I've been here thirty-five years, since the beginning. There are rules and laws that are very equalising – if you read them you'd say 'Any woman can work anywhere – any woman can do what she really wants; she doesn't have to work in the kitchen or the laundry: she can choose.' But the norm is that women have actually cut their expectations by 50 per cent. They decide to give up on 'men's jobs' even more so than outside the kibbutzim because we're a rural community. Most of us started out as city people, but living in the country has a sort of quietening effect! You're less out for change; you quietly lower your expectations. You tune yourself and your desires with what you think is possible to achieve; what's possible is actually much greater, but most of the women here give up on it . . . they narrow down and say, look, I'm going to work in education and develop a bit there. Or, I can work in laundry, in the kitchen – which are not popular jobs – I can work with clothing, sewing . . . and a lot of clerking: secretary, things like that.

Maybe some of us will think of laboratory work, nursing, and factory work – but not, say, factory work in a managerial capacity. Maybe the head of a department but not the head of a plant, you see. It's no different anywhere else, but in a kibbutz I feel that there are not as many jobs . . . you're limited by the amount of work branches you have.

Women are defining themselves as second-class citizens – our kibbutz is not such a good example because we have a very strong feeling here about sexism. Many of us are Americans, and we read English, and we're influenced more – most of the people on the kibbutz who aren't of English-speaking extraction accept the status quo quietly. When we started, other women said 'Oh, you with your women's rights' . . . There is now some committee for the advancement of women in our kibbutz movement, Kibbutz Artzi. They have meetings – I don't think anything has changed because they're not really doing anything. There are women working in education who don't want to work there; people don't see any possible alternatives.

Look – if they're thinking of doing something else, say computers, which a lot of women have gone into: we've only one computer! So what's happening is that those women who do have aspirations try to fulfil them outside. It's so limited inside the kibbutz – some find a place, some don't. So they stay, but go outside to find work – and of course, when you earn, it goes into the kibbutz funds.

I worked out of the kibbutz for many years – I'm now

teaching at a teacher's seminary. Before that I worked for seven years as a teachers' counsellor, travelling round the country to counsel teachers in other kibbutzim. So I worked for the education committee of the Kibbutz Artzi and that was a step outside our own school here, where I had taught for many years.

Of course there are men who are frustrated, too, but they have more opportunities. Now that we have an industry, there's not one woman in our factory who has a managerial position – let's say general manager, sales representative, import, export, nothing! The highest they've gone there has been the head of a small dept. When I said to a young woman whom I had taught, who has exceptionally good mathematics and who would do very well in anything to do with economics: 'Why don't you do economics?' She'd been working in the factory . . . and she said to me 'Oh, my God, I'm going to have to manage that plant? Stay there from six in the morning till twelve at night? Like the men do? I want to have a family, and children, I don't want to do it . . . it means giving up too much of yourself.

It isn't the norm for women – they are primarily responsible for their children. No matter how you look at it – and I preach to the young girls I teach, to work and find a profession – I know that I felt responsible for my children, no matter how much my husband helped me. If I studied outside of the kibbutz, I always worried to get home on time to be with the children. When he was out studying, he came home once a week! Maybe its something biological? I felt I had to do two jobs – nobody told me to; I could have stayed away. Perhaps it's a question of generations: this is the way we were educated by our mothers.

The younger generation aspire even less than we do – maybe because they're comfortable. They don't see why they should take themselves out of this peaceful life, and make life miserable for themselves . . . every advancement means taking on additional responsibilities – it doesn't only have a good part!

I teach maybe 240 girls a year; and I have two lectures that

I give them on the advancement of women; they say 'First, I'm a mother. If I work, I'll work part-time. If I have a profession, I still want to care for my children.' And every woman expects to be a wife and a mother.

We live our socialism of equal means and standards very happily – this living has its own momentum, which has given us a very nice, quiet life. I think there's something sleepy about it – it's put us women to sleep more than the men, because of our feeling of importance in the family. The women do get satisfaction out of the family . . . they have lots of hobbies, and they knit; they try to have as much leisure as possible, and they do their job on the kibbutz. Very few get into an outside political life – and if they do, it's usually before they have children; they may be very active till they have children – then the activities go down.

Very few, from the kibbutzim, have been signing up for the permanent Army in the past ten years. Most kibbutzniks will perform as well as is expected of them, and wait for the day when they can get out. My son said: 'I closed my eyes, and waited for three years to go by' – he did it because it was his duty. I could not call the youth of the kibbutzim dedicated to a military life. The new kibbutzim near the frontiers? they're established by members of one of the youth movements: the youngsters go there as part of their Army training; afterwards they stay on if they want to. There's a very big turnover . . . there was a time, like when we established Barkai, when 150 people came, and stayed for years, and made the kibbutz. It isn't like that today: today they go into the Army, they're posted to a new kibbutz and hold it and help it grow; then after their Army service some of them will go back and stay there . . . until a place like that is really settled it takes from eight to ten years.

[Talking of a new kibbutz, Geshur, in the Golan Heights]

They're not warrior-like – they're just simple agricultural settlements. The Army is there to support them, and they have their own people in the Reserve; they live very quiet, ordinary lives . . . we're very interested in having more kibbutzim, in places where we'll be able really to guard the frontier. It's been proven – as long as people live there, it belongs to us. I'm not talking about settlements on the West Bank – we're against those – but up to the Green Line. On the West Bank we have to make a political settlement, and not take land from the Arabs.

It was the kibbutz that decided I was going to be a teacher, not I; I thought, idealistically, that I had to be a farmer – very boring. Then the education committee of the kibbutz brought up my name at a meeting and said I should go to study: I came home – I was the mother of two children at that time – my youngest son was 2, my eldest 6 – and I said 'What am I going to do?' I thought it over for a month; eventually I decided someone had to be a teacher! I liked it – and I realised how much I'd missed it. So I was pushed to studying, and that led to something else, and that led to more studying . . . and another job; and even what I'm doing today, I didn't have to go out and look for it – I was asked to do it.

I feel the country is going completely right wing. So much hostility against kibbutz; and against socialism! You know – they say 'It won't work' . . . I feel it in the young people I teach at the teachers' seminary. They have just finished the Army; and I know that in the Army the percentage of soldiers that are supporting Kahane now is going up and up. Those seven years of Menachem Begin and the Likud really poisoned people's minds against the kibbutz, against socialism; against the whole co-operative ideal. Now it's every man and woman for themselves . . . but women in the second place of course.

Under Likud everybody sort of lived in this 'half-paradise' of money which we never had, of prosperity that never occurred: it was living in some false situation. People felt good, and were in a position, psychologically, to be influenced by the Right. Television programmes, radio – all forms of communication carried the message against a socialist life. You say the word socialism now, and it's become a dirty word.

I think it has something to do with the image of the

'personality' that's been created of the socialist person; someone who is living very well, a kibbutznik, living off them, not paying income tax – all sorts of lies. No matter how often we answered, and proved that the image was a false one; only a week ago, again I heard the same allegations about leftists and kibbutzniks. 'And he loves Arabs . . . all he wants to do is sell our country.' And I find this every day in my classroom . . . so those of us who care about peace with the Arabs, and about equality, have lost out . . . I didn't feel the hostility until I started teaching: you don't feel it inside the kibbutz, not to the same extent, even when you hear it on the radio . . . when I started teaching these girls; first they wouldn't say anything, but slowly and surely, as the discussions developed during the year, they became more and more open. They began to say things like that.

There's a course on democracy, a discussion course – both Arab and Jewish women attend. The discussion is very difficult – nobody wants to say anything, because they don't want to hurt each other face to face . . . and at the same time the country is becoming more racist. There's a programme here on Thursdays, on the radio – it's a discussion among young people, just before they go into the Army. There was a panel one day with three Arabs and three Jews. They were asked 'Do you feel this is your country; how do you feel here?' The Arabs, when they became honest, and they started to yell, said 'This isn't my country; I live here, but this isn't my country. And even if I think it's my country they don't think it's my country.' And the Jewish kids said to them 'There are so many other Arab countries: what do you have to stay here for?' They said 'I was born here, it's my land.' 'I'm like you, I was born here' . . . even so, the Jewish kids insisted it would be much better if they would pick up and go . . . the Arab girl said 'At the best times I feel myself like a wanted visitor, a desired visitor; at the worst times as an undesirable visitor in this country.'

The political differences between Kibbutz Barkai, which is affiliated to Mapam via its collective Kibbutz Artzi movement, and Bet Ha Emek, a kibbutz near the Lebanese border that's a member of the United Kibbutz Movement and a supporter of the Ma'arach Labour grouping in the Knesset, are about what kind and what degree of welfare socialism they believe in, and the impact that has on the daily lives of Jews and Arabs in Israel and beyond. But life styles on the kibbutzim are also different; Bet Ha Emek was the first kibbutz in Israel to decide, some years ago, that it no longer wanted collective sleeping arrangements for its under-14 year olds. The change has meant a lot of rebuilding, as family bungalows were extended to take the children: it has also created the need for one parent to be at home when young children return from school or nursery. It is a growing trend. Paradoxically, in spite of the tighter family unit here, the women on the two kibbutzim continue to have very much the same roles. And where the Barkai women are at times disconsolate about their lot, my impression at Bet Ha Emek was one of contentment among the younger women. At this kibbutz, Trudi endorses her position very positively, because she feels it gives her greater involvement in her children's lives. She feels privileged to be able to spend more time with her four children than her husband, and endorses the biology-determines-destiny argument by saying that whoever does the first parenting is central to the child's life; she does the breast-feeding, and from that all follows. Trudi mainly wants power, because it will help her determine the choices and the future, on the kibbutz, for her children.

> If a woman chooses to have a family, that's her first responsibility. Yes, because the child needs his mother: if he grows up deprived of his mother, he's not going to be a responsible adult, he's not going to be able to cope. I don't think fathers could do this work as well as mothers . . . first of all, I breast-feed my children till they're about a year old. The contact between a mother and child – no father can do it – unless only the father looks after him from the minute the baby's born, but that never happens.
>
> If I look after my baby until it's five or six months old, and then I decide I want to go out to work and my husband says,

'All right, I'll stay at home and I'll do the cooking and I'll look
after the baby' – I'm depriving my baby. It's *me* the child
needs because I was the first contact.

I don't feel that women should take some of the
responsibilities on the kibbutz, not if it's going to take them
away from the children. The only way it could work would be
if my husband were to take over the day the baby was born. If
I'm the secretary of the kibbutz, which I could very well be,
I'm sure, that would mean in the afternoon I would be away;
my kids would come home and there'd be no mother there. I
wouldn't be able to put them to bed, I wouldn't be able to sit
and tell them a story, because I'd be too busy. No, I wouldn't
do that.

A woman in town, if her husband goes out to work, she
stays at home all day long – I can see she's going to feel
resentful. He goes out to his job, ,and he meets his friends and
he has a full day. She just sits home and does the housework,
and waits for him to come home.

I wouldn't like that at all, but I don't have that kind of life. I
go out, I have a responsible job on the kibbutz, I meet people;
then in the afternoon, I'm with my children – that's what I
choose, that's what I want.

Her mother, Ethel, says that when she first came to Bet Ha
Emek she asked to work with the cows but was not allowed
because that was considerd a man's job. 'And they wouldn't let
me ride the tractor because they said my womb would be
spoiled.' There are two women working in the cowshed now;
someone else who wanted to learn carpentry, another male
domain, was allowed to start and then continually criticised.
Ethel says, 'Judy got no help at all – the very opposite. She fitted
out a room for me – I was working in cosmetics – with shelves
and cupboards, and she did it very well indeed. A man carpenter
came and he just sneered "Who did that work, for goodness
sake?"' Judy no longer works in the carpentry shop . . . but the
younger women on the kibbutz mostly support service work for
their sisters and themselves anyway.

Back at Barkai, there are also frustrations about inequality.
Dvora Snitz:

There aren't any men ironing! And you know what, if a woman breaks a leg, and she has a convalescence period, she'll go and iron. We made a stink about it, not too long ago – there was a guy that broke his leg and he was lying at home! He was lying at home . . . finally, that was too much, it was too obvious: after we made the fuss he went to do some office work, sat by the phone – then we insisted he go to iron!

The kibbutz, as well as Israel itself, is seen by some as a refuge from the anti-semitism that shadowed their lives elsewhere. Tamar Livney, just 19 and about to start her Army service:

For 2,000 years they've been trying to destroy us. When I lived in New Jersey I was beaten at school and at the Girl Scouts – I was beaten by kids in the fifth grade; I was pushed about until I got to the point where I didn't go out at recess. I'd be pushed in the hallway and someone would shout 'Jew'. Now I belong here.

Most of the young women on the kibbutz don't want to go into the Army – they find that most women only serve coffee and do filing, which is boring. I think the thing to do is to try and go for more important things like being a social worker, or working with people, perhaps as a counsellor.

Personally I feel I have to go into the Army· I wasn't born here and I want to do something for my country that'll help: help the Army, the safety of the country. I've been on the kibbutz for eight years – we came from America; of course I'm an Israeli today.

The life of young men and young women on the kibbutz is basically no different except in work. In work there is a difference, because physically we are weaker; we don't have the muscle to do everything, so for example you could have guys loading boxes and girls cleaning up the kibbutz . . . some of the girls have complained, saying it's chauvinistic, but it was arranged by those who draw up the work list. That's a man and a woman together, by the way. If women complain about being given 'female' jobs, they're given a chance: if a girl complains 'Why you guys are loading boxes, and girls don't?', they send her out to load boxes if she really wants to.

After the Army I'll come back to the kibbutz for nine months as part of my contract; then I'll get 3,000 dollars to do whatever I want – travelling, learning. Usually people do leave the kibbutz for a while to learn what the outside life is like. I find that more kibbutzniks travel around to learn about work in the city. But as I know a lot of people from the outside world, I pretty much know what it's like. I'd like to do it, too, but I'm rather doing it to see places and meet people. That means much more to me, personally. Then I'll come back to the kibbutz. Actually, I'll probably go to another kibbutz where the children sleep at home until they reach first or second grade [seven or eight years old]. I spent two years in the Children's House here. It was fun – I was 11, 12 in the Children's House. But when I look at the younger kids, I think they need their parents a little more. They want to spend time with their parents . . . and its important to their personality; and I think it's also important to the mother and father.

Yes, I think I will spend the rest of my life on a kibbutz, but rather one where *my* children will be with me till a certain age; then I like the idea of them growing up together – it's beautiful. It also gives the women more freedom, because there aren't that many chores at home; and also, because in most cases it's the woman who feels obligated to spend more time with the child. At 14 I went into the High School – we became a bigger boarding group as the school is shared with three other kibbutzim. That's a good thing – I learnt a lot about other people; how to be considerate . . . the High School is set up in such a way that you learn more about kibbutz life; we lived on a mini kibbutz, that's what it really is.

Increasingly, on the kibbutz, people live together before they marry. If they request married quarters, they get them. In most cases, each person has their room and they move into one of them. No one asks any questions. . . . The Pill is readily available, free on the kibbutz. And there's counselling and sexual education in the High School. After their first child most women go on to the IUD. We have abortion available on demand – if you're under 18 your parents have to sign for it. No one usually knows about it . . . first you'd go to the gynaecologist in Hadera; then it's worked out. There's no problem, like there is for religious women in the cities.

Right now I'm teaching a group of kids from the United States how to put their money together in order to buy a big cake to celebrate their first birthday here. They've never lived collectively, and its hard for them to accept that – giving in their money. I have to keep it in the bank for them. People in the city don't realise how we do it; they think, you know, we just work and get all these things, and the government helps us. I think, in a way, we're richer just because we're a large community and enjoy each other's company. And we can get around. Even 14-year-olds learn how the finances of the kibbutz work. Most children know how things work, and who's head of the kibbutz. Its important to know; we live here: most of us are going to live here for the rest of our lives.

Even at 19 I feel I'm taking part, in a small way, in the running of the kibbutz. I feel I'm doing the best I can. Working is part of it; when people turn to me from different committees, I help – I might perform on the stage, or help with decorations; I help out with ideas. Or people come to me to help with children, being a counsellor or giving a lecture. Or helping out so that some volunteers, like the kids from the States, can understand about the kibbutz . . . nobody can ever give their full part, but for my age, its fairly full! I'm doing the best I can . . . and I accept responsibility: we all do. Everybody realises that if people weren't responsible, it wouldn't work. No way could this place work – and it's a happy place.

Mitzi came to Barkai at a much later age; an age when a kibbutz would normally no longer take new members, but only the parents of members. She was 50; and she's chosen what some might call 'women's work' – but she doesn't see it that way at all . . .

I'm certainly not just a washerwoman; it's being what one might call a 'laundry technician' – one has to know the fabrics and sort clothing; one has to work and maintain the machines; and one has to know how to organise the work.

Two people wash for 500 people. We do the day-to-day
maintenance as well as the monthly maintenance ourselves. If
there's a minor breakdown we also do the repair work on the
washing machines and boilers. In the folding of the laundry
and repair work, darning and mending, it's 99–100 per cent
women. Sometimes when some guy breaks his leg or hurts
his back, he might sit here and help for a few days, but
usually it's just women who do this work. I accept that there
are some jobs that men won't do, simply because the folding
and the ironing doesn't require much physical strength. It's
very often done by older women, pregnant women, people
like that. It's not regular work for people at full strength, so
to speak.

I find it challenging because it involves all sorts of
things – both mechanical and organisational aspects,
knowledge and skill in fabrics, in the chemistry of laundry. I
went on a five-day course on chemistry, and the taking out of
stains. That's a very skilled job which, in places like the
Hilton Hotel – there's a guy there whose been working on
that for 20 years – just working on stains. It's satisfying
work, organisationally – how to get the work out to the
people on the kibbutz in an organised manner, so that they
can plan their day and do what they have to do, and not just
send it to them without any order . . . it requires some skill.
There are two people washing the clothing for 500; another
six or seven who are folding, ironing and mending. Most
people wash out their brassières, let's say, but we do most
everything here – very delicate fabrics, underpants: we'll
wash anything and everything.

When I first came here, one of the things I did in
addition to working as the person in charge of the dining
room was to teach English to fifth and sixth grade students.
And two afternoons a week, for about four months, I
worked in Adda, which is an Arab village about 8 kilometres
from here. I taught English to a group of Arab teachers and
nurses. That was through the Mapam; the relationships were
very good. At that time we had all sorts of study circles with
Arabs – somebody went and taught cooking, and so on.

Today there's nobody doing that . . . for a long time this kibbutz had a group called Interns for Peace – for six years, and we had joint activities between classes with the Arab students. My personal relationships with Arabs are on a very very limited basis.

No Arab has ever applied to be a member of the kibbutz. We had Arabs living in the kibbutz – participating in the Interns for Peace programme; but that was also questioned. It came before the general meetings: there was a question about an Arab girl: what if she became pregnant here; then the whole Arab community would blame us. There was a whole discussion about whether we should or should not accept Arab men. People were concerned not so much about terrorism as sabotage even though these were people who had voluntarily gone into a programme of joint Arab/Jewish co-operation. There was still anxiety; not overwhelmingly. And the general meeting had overwhelmingly approved that they should be here, but the anxiety remained.

A POSTSCRIPT

Kibbutz Barkai has never had an Arab member. Here Havah Halevi, who also grew up on a Hashomei Hatzair kibbutz – one in the northern Sharon near Barkai – tells a relevant story.

The name of the village was Sarkas, which probably refers to the former origin of its inhabitants, Circassians, who came, I don't know how, to the Middle East and settled here. Anyway, when I came to know the village, all of its inhabitants were Palestinian-Arabs. In fact, I never came properly to know the village; I was never there, though this is only half the truth, and I shall return to that later.

In our eyes, the eyes of children 4 or 5 years old, the village was represented by two women, Khadija and Hanifa. Maybe they were more courageous than the rest, or maybe they served as something like the 'Foreign Office' of the village. They often walked about in the kibbutz, and as far as

I can remember they were mainly preoccupied with the picking of khubeiza (mallow) leaves which grew in wild abundance along the roadside. When we asked why they pick the khubeiza we were told that the Arabs cook the leaves and eat them. And so, the first thing I ever knew about Arabs was that they eat khubeiza. I also knew, of course, that they ride on camels, since the camels used to pass through the kibbutz and occasionally camp there; I knew that they ride on donkeys along the white road which probably stretches up to the very end of the world. But at that time there were in the area also British soldiers [the Mandate] and also Australian soldiers, and thus it was embedded in my consciousness that Eretz Israel consists of us, as well as passersby: Arab, British, Australians . . .

About that time they all disappeared, and I really did not notice their disappearance all that much. Of course, the departure of the British was accompanied by much talk on the radio and in the yard of the kibbutz. But as to the fact that Khadija and Hanifa ceased to show up — well, there are many events that pass through the universe of any child, and he or she may accept their appearance as well as their disappearance as a matter of fact. Later I came to know that the village was destroyed with bulldozers, and I was a little scared. And then I forgot, and many years passed before Sarkas again emerged before my eyes as a place where people lived.

The destroyed village was made into the kibbutz garbage dump. I do not know who was the first to discover that in the midst of the ruins and the dust and the stench there remained a mulberry tree. A huge mulberry tree, which, in summer produced huge mulberries: black and deliciously sweet. The mulberry trees in the kibbutz were grown on much water and their fruit was therefore somewhat watery, and anyway they were much too high to climb on. But this mulberry tree was low, spreading wide, and heavily laden with fruit to the deep delight of a little girl who was rather quiet and clumsy and who loved mulberries. And thus, every Saturday we would go on pilgrimage to the mulberry tree, stand around it for hours and eat of its fruit and return home with hands and faces blackened by the dark dye of mulberry sap. Never, not once, while standing there among the ruins and the dust under the scathing sun did we talk or think of the inhabitants of Sarkas who lived here: where are they? where did they go? why?

In 1961 a very young woman from kibbutz Gib'at ha-Sheloshah married an Arab youth, Rashid Masarwa who was employed in her kibbutz. The kibbutz refused to allow them to remain there, and they applied to join my kibbutz. The debate on whether they were to be admitted or whether they were not to be admitted extended over one and a half years and shook the kibbutz in a way that no other subject did ever before or since. The debate cut across families, and brought sons to rebel against their parents, brothers against brothers and husbands against wives. The leadership of Hashomer Hatzair kibbutz federation was called to present its position (opposed) and threats of leaving the kibbutz on this matter were voiced in both camps. In the end the 'mixed couple' were not admitted to the kibbutz. Both camps were already tired of endless debates and rows. In a bitter discussion which I (who had supported their admission) had with one of the leading opponents he told me: 'Do you know that Rashid is a son of the village of Sarkas? Do you think he can live here, raise here his children and always see across the street the hill which was his village *and not think anything?*'

At that moment, together with the scorching sun and the dust I felt in my mouth the taste of mulberries, and I understood what homeland means, and also, for the first time, vaguely and at a distance and a little bit afraid, I understood that this homeland, the homeland of the songs and the school textbooks, is simply just the taste of mulberries, and the smell of dust, and the moist earth in winter, and the colour of the sky, and that it is a homeland not only for me but also for Rashid Masarwa. At that very moment, in the midst of the heated discussion, the taste of mulberries and the shock, I remembered one fearful memory:

It was towards the end of the 1948 war, after we had won the war and defeated the Arab armies and had a state of our own. We were lying in bed. Eight children in the children's house (right in the centre of the kibbutz so that we would be safe). It was night. From the distance we heard the heavy and rumbling noise. It was not very far away, but one could clearly hear that the noise did not come from inside the kibbutz. And the noise went on and on and on. I asked what was this protracted continuous noise, and one of the children told me that two kibbutz members went with bulldozers to Sarkas to destroy the houses of the Arabs. In real fear of Arab revenge, I asked: 'But what will the Arabs do when they come back and see that we have destroyed their home?' And then he answered: 'This is why we destroy their homes, so that they do not come back.'

I then knew that the matter was lost. The home of Rashid was destroyed then in order that he did not return. In order that he, his mother in the long black robe who walks erect with the bundle of wood magnificently balanced on her head, and all his brothers and sisters who run barefoot on the stones, do not return. And also now they will not let him come back.

CHAPTER 9

SOME ARE STATELESS IN GAZA

If a young man is arrested for a resistance act, we can disagree on that – they call it terrorism, I call it resistance because every human being has the right to resist occupation. Okay, we can disagree on that, and that's no harm. We can never disagree, as human beings, that the house of that young man, that contains all the family – children, mother, father, everybody – should be demolished; that's against all human rights. That's a rape, not just a violation.

Mary Khass works for the United Nations relief organisation, UNRWA, among the hundreds of thousands of refugees from Israel who have lived in the camps of Gaza since 1948. We had travelled in her car along the dirt roads of the Jabalia camp – where the sewage flows freely – to visit the Emsalem family. Mo'en Emsalem had been arrested two weeks earlier, soon after being released from five and a half years imprisonment. At the time of his first arrest, the family home had been demolished. I opened the packing case gate into a neatly swept, sandy compound hedged by prickly pear bushes and more packing cases. In the centre, an obstinate stub of prefabricated breeze block a foot high marked the outline of the demolished house: above it there was more cardboard, tin and a tentcloth. An ancient fig tree provided some shade; underneath, its flex trailing through the branches, an old washing machine spun, churning the clothes to be rinsed in two twin-tubs nearby.

The Emsalems welcomed us with fizzy orangeade and prickly pears. There has been dysentery, typhoid and even cholera in the overcrowded camp and they did not trust the local standpipes for drinking water. Their daughter Qifah had broken off her engagement at Mo'en's re-arrest, and now her fiancé, too, had been detained. Mo'en, found guilty in 1981 of attacking Israeli installations, had been put inside this time because he objected to the six Israeli soldiers who had sat at the gate for days, guns on their knees and impugning – he felt – the honour of his six sisters.

Mary Khass has worked in the Gaza area for many years.

> It is the women who pay, when this happens. In a crisis, and especially under occupation, it is the woman who pays the price. She is the person who has to put up with the cleaning, the trying to keep the children healthy when all are now living in a tent and almost in the street. She is the one who suffers when her son is in prison, who stands by her husband and supports him if he is in prison. She takes over.

Mary, who went to school in Haifa with Jewish as well as Arab friends, has never given up trying to talk to others about Arab needs and desires.

> For many years now I've been dialoguing with Jewish people. The dialogue we had in Nairobi was objective simply because we were able to address women living outside Israel as well as Israeli women. They heard the Palestinian voice from Palestinains themselves and realised that, living under occupation, we can still feel and think humanly and not fanatically. I was able to express that. I do care what happens to the Israeli people; they felt that and I was able to share my own experience under occupation with them, and it moved them.
>
> From the beginning I told them: you have been through miseries, oppression, discrimination and then finally the holocaust. We've taken that trip. That should make us friends: we should put our hands together and try to struggle against that kind of regime. Remember, it has a reaction on your community as Jewish people too. War is not a one-sided sword; it is two-edged. It is making fanatics on both sides.

The men are taking action because of their profound frustration. The world comes to pay attention, under our kind of occupation, only when there is a crisis but, believe me, what happens daily – the frustrations of the daily happenings – is so humiliating, so oppressive that even I, as a non-violent person, become very angry. . . .

In the old days, before the 1967 occupation, it was inside Israel that the worst economic situation existed – the first who paid, in bad times, were the Arabs in Israel, the Palestinians inside the Green Line. Then came the Oriental Jews; by then a temporary economic solution would have been found (often by developing the arms industry)[1] and very few of the elite, the Ashkenazi, would suffer. Nowadays it starts with the workers under occupation – they're the ones to pay the price; then come the Arabs in Israel, then again the Oriental Jews. Even in the Knesset and the Histadrut you hear the voices – Why should the Palestinians under occupation take the jobs from the pure, from the Jewish people?

Workers who leave Gaza every day to work within Israel live in a very large prison – it's worse than South Africa. A prison that they leave early in the morning and come back to late at night. They are totally at the mercy of their employer – and here, in Gaza, we are not allowed any development, it's forbidden. We've tried, very hard: it's forbidden. They don't want us to compete with Israeli industry, and also, they think, it makes control easier.

There's an employment office here, run by the occupying authority. It's not for the benefit of the workers, it's for the authorities, so that they know who works inside Israel. They also do it for the – quote unquote – security of Israel; Arab workers are not allowed to sleep, to stay overnight in Israel – once they're registered it's easy enough to check.

But this turned out to be catastrophic, because some of the

1 Israel makes jet fighters like the Kfir. It has developed tanks, rifles, missiles and also a nuclear strategy based on installations in the Negev desert. It is the world's fourth most powerful military power.

employees work evenings and nights. The bosses had to give guarantees to the authority that they would take care of these people and be responsible for their movements.

Their understanding of taking care of them was to lock them in and a few catastrophic events took place: one time a fundamentalist Kahanist threw a bomb at the workers; another time there was an electric short and two of them died. Then there was the occasion when one developed appendicitis, and died.

The women work mainly in the nearby settlements, or on the kibbutzim on vegetable allotments: they come back daily. Both men and women do unskilled work. According to Dayan's plan – his speech in the Knesset, when he advised that the gates of the occupied territories be opened: he said, 'We will open the gates, so that they have something to do, instead of fighting and resisting and dying'. It was one way of trying to absorb resistance in the occupied territory. For security reasons, they are only allowed to be *black labourers*. In Hebrew, that means unskilled workers . . . and that's how it is. Even the skilled labourers have to do unskilled work, simply because they are not offered anything else.

We sat quietly next to the fig tree in the heat, to dust off the dry sand. I remembered the open trucks full of soldiers that I had seen in the streets of Gaza that morning, mounted machine guns on a swivel, rifles ready . . . nineteen yeras after the area had been taken over from the Egyptians, it still felt like war rather than occupation. 'Camp people call it the second Vietnam,' Mary said. 'They do not accept the occupation. Many of the boys and girls are in prison.' The centre of Gaza is called Palestine Square: perhaps an irony today when the word has such a guilt-by-association with the PLO for so many Israelis.

Because the men feel so threatened, and because we women are not taken seriously by any regime, let alone an occupying authority, we are able to do a lot for the community. I like to call it Woman community development, the crèches and the clinics we start . . . fifty years ago most of the world was as my people are now, but they had their chance, they had their freedom. In their own country they were able to make some progress under a government that they had elected. We have been under Turkish occupation, British, Egyptian and now Israeli: we have not had the possibilities and the atmosphere for development.

That's why we must realise our own independence as women as well as that of our people; and because the men are under such pressure from the occupation they are actually making more room for us because of it . . . they are beginning to share power with us, to accept us as leaders as well as partners in the community. They enjoy it; I think they're sometimes overwhelmed by what they see, by our capacity!

The statistics on Gaza, the tiny 140-square mile strip that abuts Egypt and the Sinai desert as well as Israel, are a recital of misery and deprivation. 700,000 people, most of them in 40-year-old refugee camps with completely inadequate conditions, live in the most overcrowded conditions known anywhere. Unlike the Arabs of the West Bank, they have no right to any passport and their earning potential is also far lower. The Israeli academic who has documented settler and Arab conditions on the West Bank, Dr Meron Benvenisti, has also now completed a study of Gaza: he details a system of 'discrimination and injustice' where income is actually declining as it rises for the 2,000 Jewish settlers in the area.

Dr Benvenisti has calculated that the Israeli government owes Gaza's stateless refugees 500 million dollars as their contribution to the Israeli economy over twenty years of occupation. Squashed as they are into the most densely populated area in the world, they must find it ironic that the World Zionist Organisation's immigration and absorption division has recently called the pocket handkerchief territory the 'Hawaii of Israel'. New Jewish settlers do not draw water from the contaminated wells or standpipes and they also have their own beaches.

Under the original UN partition plan for Palestine in 1947, Gaza was designated part of a new Palestinian state, but it was occupied and administered by Egypt in 1948–1967: then, too, there was no economic development. The signing of the Camp David agreement in 1978 means that Gaza has no Arab connections of any kind, and its citizens have no Israeli rights either. They cannot travel because they have no passports.

Mary Khass says, 'We have to find a way, any way, to stop the expansion of Jewish settlements and the confiscation of Arab land. While the world waits Israel goes on creating new facts.' In Jabalia, the waiting has become explosive.

In the flat white heat, Lea Tsemel's high-ceilinged office is cool and pleasant. A dozen people sit and stand in the waiting room, listening quietly to the lawyer's talk drifting through the open door to her office. They – men and women – are dressed in Sunday best, the men with suits under their flowing robes, the older women with fresh silk or cotton scarves around their heads. Lea, a former Zionist, is now the busiest solicitor in East Jerusalem working on the defence of those arrested or detained by the military administration in Gaza and the West Bank. In her husky voice she discusses Achmed Abbadee's case with his mother: Achmed has been in gaol three months, charged with membership of a Palestinian organisation; at last the case is going to trial. 'I think he may have thrown stones, but he had nothing to do with the gun,' says Mrs Abbadee.

Lea, 40 and Jewish, speaks fluent Arabic. She talks to a young science teacher who has been unable to get any information about her husband, or have any access to him, since his detention two months ago. The teacher is insistent: please, please find him and press for charges or release. (Lea has already handled dozens of cases of this sort and many detainees are held for up to six months, to be released again without any charges having been brought.) There's a sudden rustle of papers and the quiet voices rise slightly. Lea appears, ready to drive to the military court in Ramallah, 15 miles away. It is already a quarter past nine and the court sits in fifteen minutes: in spite of that the mothers, fathers, wives and daughters in the waiting room plead for attention . . . another five minutes and a rush down the stairs to the Fiat parked outside. There is a black and white kuffiyya (Arab headscarf) on the floor of the car, and as we leave for the West Bank Lea places it in a prominent place on the front windscreen – her yellow Israeli numberplates could mean stones thrown on the drive to court, even for Lea Tsemel.

I have to visit the prison today, as well as go to court: there are some political prisoners to whom I've been granted access. I take only political cases – there are other lawyers who do this work too, but we are all very busy. I'd say that nearly everyone in Gaza or the West Bank who is over 16 has been detained or interrogated at least once but women are only 1 per cent of the Palestinian prisoners at any one time – about 30 of the present 3,000. I get to meet them when they have problems, or when their sons or husbands have them.

I often see women because during the years of occupation they have become the most active ones over the everyday problems of detention. They go to the police, they ask for permits – it's not traditional, but they have become very active; they take the responsibility on themselves. They're more stubborn than the men – they will not be satisfied with a lower policeman, and they don't feel so much threatened when they go to the police station.

It's in the nature of the occupation that the women are coming out from behind the veil, out of their homes, in a way that modesty has never allowed under the Muslim tradition. High School girls take part today in demonstrations, undoubtedly breaking the orders of the family, the patriarchic structure of the family . . . a woman participating in a demonstration or throwing stones, expecting to be arrested, that's not a normal thing but here the girls do it.

Muslim women traditionally stay at home: they should not be exposed to the public, they should be private property . . . now even the peasant women go out. For their children they will do anything, including going to the police and the lawyers, and taking part in the demonstrations. They have also been on strike in prison, in the Red Cross centres, and they visit those who are in prison even when their own sons are released.

We arrive at a long, low military building. It looks like a British barracks, painted white; and so it was until 1948. Will they let me into the military court? I walk quietly next to Lea, eyes down, as she greets and smiles at uniforms in all directions. The courtroom is small, with a raised wooden dais for the judge or magistrate. Everything else is painted a shiny warship grey and there's a stove with a tin chimney going through the wall. On the benches for the relatives of defendants sits a thin young woman in black, a silk scarf around her hair. She is dejected and she looks exhausted, a hand to her head. It is ten o'clock.

Lea puts on her gown and talks to the young woman. The court fills up with men and women in Arab dress and men and women in Israeli uniform; all, that is, except me, cautiously holding the thinnest of thin notebooks in my hands and still afraid someone will notice and order me out.

An officer in uniform enters and goes to the dais and the proceedings start in a jumble of Hebrew, Arabic and – another defending solicitor – English. No one seems to mind. The young Druze translator is so short, so boxed in between the witness stand and a high-backed chair, that he can't actually see the prosecutor when he turns to hear what is being said. He never waits for the end of a sentence, but does a virtually simultaneous translation from Hebrew and English into Arabic. Lea, firmly, politely, begins plea-bargaining ... the soldiers lining the wall are sleepy; one creeps out of the room, pulling a cigarette pack from his pocket. Lea agrees that her client made the Molotov cocktail, but it was never thrown: two years is too long. The translator rushes into her words and the sentence is reduced slightly. The sentence on the next defendant, brother to the thin young woman and also, since the death of their other brother in an explosion from a home-made hand grenade, responsible for the dead man's six children, is deferred. We break for lunch.

Lea was born in Haifa.

My parents came from Russia and Poland. In the 1967 war – I was totally unpolitical – I came to believe that there would finally be peace. Then, when it didn't happen, when I saw the treatment of the Palestinian population, then all my questions came. What was here in '48? And I lost my illusions about the Independence war. What the Jews were doing then, in the original areas of the partitioned State, they're doing on the West Bank now. And now they're facing the fact that the Palestinians didn't escape, and they will have to swallow that whole population.

I think they'd rather have the land of the West Bank without the population. Of course there are divisions in the Zionist movement: there are those who say 'We cannot do it', due to their humanistic background, but there are clearly others – not only Kahane and his supporters – who would like to 'get rid of' the one million people who live here. Then there are those who want a Partition -- a separate State for Palestinians and a separate State for Jews. Some would like to do it by force. I should like to live in the same State, but equally.

I decided to do this job because of the evils that exist . . . I'm not popular with the police; there are problems with new policemen and soldiers when we first met: they have to get used to this phenomenon. The consequences are stronger for my children. They go to regular Israeli schools, in Jerusalem. At school there's no discrimination at the formal level, but whenever there's a fight among the children my son is told 'your mother is a Fatah, she's a terrorist'. My daughter is still too young, so nothing has happened to her yet.

When I met Amal Wahadan her electrician husband was town arrested and unable to pursue his daily work. Amal is an accountant and has a 2-year-old daughter, Leana.

I opened my eyes under the occupation. I was 9 years old and in third grade when I began to see the demonstrations against occupation; I see the Israeli soldiers with their weapons chasing kids or students, arresting them, spraying them with coloured water to identify them so that they can take them easily to the police station for interrogation. Then I grow up, as any child in this country, seeing all the practices of the Israeli soldiers against the inhabitants, against the Palestinian people. Living under curfew, the arrest of my brother once because he was playing with a wooden toy gun – also my mother running after them begging them to leave her boy. They took him for two nights and afterwards my parents, as a response to this – they were afraid their child would be hurt – decided to send him away and out of the country. At that time I realised that my brother would not be away from me if there was no occupation; in school I began participating in all the demonstrations – I'm sure as a result of what happened with my brother. I want my country to be free: I want all my brothers and my sister, my relatives to come back to their country, and to live in their country without being arrested, without being pushed away. Because of the occupation, all that I have here is my mother now . . .

We used to demonstrate against Jordan, before the Israeli occupation – not me, I was too young. The Jordanian regime was also very harsh on us, using all aggressive ways to suppress the Palestinian people.

I used to have suppression from my parents, my mother and my father, but also from the people around – they don't like the woman who is alone in the street, or who has activities or friends outside. Our part in the society is to change it and to improve our position.

We know our freedom of movement or participating with the men in the liberation of our country can't be easily taken: we have to fight to have our freedom; our social and our political freedom. And myself, I had so many problems, with my family, with the neighbours, with the relatives, because I used to go on demonstrations, I used to work together with my colleagues and my male friends at the University – so I have had to fight on different fronts to achieve my positon.

The social values have changed quite a lot since 1967: women have started to go out to work – and outside their home. They work in factories and schools; in some places the chance to get work has improved and men accept it because of the economic need. People in the countryside have had to leave their lands because they cannot compete with the Israeli product, and go and work for wages – many of them inside Israel.

Thousands of workers from the West Bank and the Gaza Strip work 'invisibly' – without the permission of the Works Ministry and the labour exchange. 120,000 men and 33,000–34,000 women. We believe our main struggle though, is among women who live at home. Those who go out have the chance to meet with people, exchange ideas, but women in their houses are those who are in much greater need.

Women have unlimited capabilities, as we've seen in some societies; we are capable of great efforts – but we need the chance to use our capabilities in the right way; then we're able to do as well as the man. My hope is to see a society where the men and the women together work to build it, with no differences of sex, with no differences in whatever. If both have their mind, their capabilities: we need a social system in which we can use them. We have quite a fight – in our culture men are so dominant! I was very lucky: my husband believes, as I do, in women's liberation and in our role in the society.

If I'm not at home he can change Leana's diapers. He can feed her. I can say he understands equality: we can arrange it between ourselves that when I am busy he takes care of her, he takes care of the house. On the other hand, if he is busy I take care of his role. We have no difficulties.

I've been under town arrest for two months; I was pregnant at the time and I had a case in the court. I was living in a village south of Jerusalem, five kilometres square. I couldn't leave the village; I had to be at home at night: they used to come and check whether I was at home or not. I had to go each week to the police station at Bethlehem, about 25 kilometres from the village, to prove my residency. If visitors came to the home, they were watched, my telephone tapped; all kinds of solidarity visits were known to the secret police. At the beginning I had too many troubles, because I was pregnant at the time and I had visits to the doctor – at that time my husband was in Gaza prison: I had to visit him as well every two weeks. Then I raised a case against town arrest and finally succeeded in getting the order removed.

We do have contacts with Jewish women – in general I believe in strengthening our links with them, in the growth of co-operation between the two sides. I have a lot of Israeli friends and they helped me a lot when I was under town arrest, talking to the Jewish public. I suppose that as a Palestinian I would like to see independent States in the West Bank and Gaza, but I think, as a whole view, that we'd all be better off living together in a united democratic country. I hope for a future where Jews and Palestinians can live with equality and rights in spite of religious beliefs, sex roles or any other kind of differences. I'm talking about a secular State with religious freedom, where we can solve religious problems and all can practice their own beliefs. Do you think it can ever come? . . .

CHAPTER 10

AN ENDING –
THE VOICE OF REASON?

Wherever I had gone, the women I met had been eager to talk about both their own lives, the roles in which they had been cast by custom, religion and tradition, and about their felt perceptions of life in the more general – and especially political – range. The two areas seemed disparate at first; what, for example, could a whole set of military and political decisions about Lebanon have to do with women who were sitting at home but feeling far from mutinous about that? Why should Arab women feel their political work and aspirations to be so closely linked with coming out of that home? Gradually my impressions clarified: the unities that emerged, clustered around power and religion, suggested that those women who cared most about rights and freedom in this small country were also those most concerned that women should have the opportunity to grow to parity with men. Those who were most religious – Arab or Jew – accepted with the greatest alacrity the subservient role that God or Allah or some of their subsequent sages had decreed for women. Many of the Orthodox, too, did not appear to care as passionately about the rights of all the people of Israel, or the West Bank, or Gaza (wherever they happened to be living) as long as their own present status and power were not impugned. I met fear, a great deal of hatred, but also tolerance and concern between the two major groups. Overwhelmingly, the Right appears to be advancing and the voice of reason is muted, tense and on the defensive. That cannot be good for women or the body politic. If, then, these connections exist between women's lives and the general

situation, it means that the personal statements ought to close
on a political note.

Judy Levitan, who earlier spoke of her concern about
religious customs that are forced on those who are secular in
their beliefs, addresses herself to the wider theme.

I do feel some sort of responsibility towards Israel, towards
the feeling that somebody has to fight for a place where Jews
can feel it is their own country. It's a problem of course,
because coming to Israel after two thousand years, people
were living here – and they didn't like the idea at all. So what
do you do? Do you abandon the idea, or do you fight? I
recognise that the founding of the Israeli State is unjust to the
Arabs. Only if two people need the same thing they have to
share it somehow to find a solution . . . I can't say bluntly
that because the Arabs were here then the Jews don't have
any right to the land . . . there isn't a clean outright solution
which will satisfy everybody.

There has been no genuine sharing between Arab and Jew
since 1948. But then the Palestinian Arabs weren't so easy to
cope with either and the Arab countries are hostile to Israel,
which you can understand on the one hand but you don't
like on the other. I mean nobody wants to sit there to be
slaughtered or pushed to the sea, which they said they were
going to do to Israel. So there was a necessity to build up a
strong Army . . . the problems began when it started to get
out of hand and instead of being a defending Army, it
became a conquering Army. Maybe in a way it started right
from the beginning, because Zionism is like a supermarket
basket with anything and everything in it . . . some of the
Zionists are peaceful people looking for a solution for the
Arabs, while others aren't – it depends who you are looking
at. But of course it was accelerated with the Six Day
War . . . it was accelerated because the Palestinians came
under military law, and aggression on both sides grows more
tense all the time. And then the Palestinians have organised
much better. I think the Arab countries have changed their
attitudes. In the beginning they weren't really supporting the

PLO, they were only exploiting it for their own interests, but now it's grown to a force which nobody can deny a place somehow.

The whole situation is so complicated; in its own logic it's already unjust. I hate the aggressiveness, the imperialistic ideas of the government. I can't bear what's going on in the West Bank and Gaza – it's utterly foreign to me. It's not only that I oppose it politically; I also don't understand these people in the Army, I have nothing in common with them. I find it much easier to share ideas and values with Arabs than with these Jewish military lunatics from the West Bank. But still I can't say Okay – Israel shouldn't exist . . . sometimes I doubt whether it will continue to exist: the lunatics could bring the destruction of Israel, and that's also something I really hold against them.

It aggravates me terribly: these people didn't build the country. It was a lot of other people, with very different ideas, who built the country and gave the best years, and sometimes their lives.

It's not only the military, but also those people in the settlements, the Gush Emunim: they're doing harm to Israel, they're doing harm to me, and if Israel collapses I'm going to collapse even though I take no share in the responsibility.

Before Israel can take any real steps towards a relationship with Palestinian Arabs we need to undergo a change – at the moment Jewishness and Judaism is a way of pointing out who is inside the group and who is outside . . . how can even an Israeli Arab feel anything towards the country when all the symbols are so rooted in the Jewish heritage and not in anything humanistic?

I think Israeli Jews are really terrified, terrified about everything . . . they can't find themselves and they get more and more aggressive and more preoccupied. They put everyone into categories, into their own box . . . how can there be any possibility for a relationship with the Arabs when Jews themselves, secular and religious, can't even come to terms with each other?

I want a democratic, secular Israel: a modern State, that's

all. That would be one way of being able to live with the Israeli Arabs, and maybe even with the Palestinians, in one political system. A political system is, after all, only a mechanism, no more, no less.

Rasha is the pseudonym of a young Arab woman who lives in Israel. She was educated abroad as a scientist and now works on the West Bank, returning every evening to her home in Israel, in contrast to the thousands of Arabs from Gaza and the West Bank who find their daily bread in Israel. Rasha has asked to remain anonymous because she knows that in taping this frank interview, she could be open to charges on a number of issues.

Look, how can I tell you the truth about our lives? If I mention the PLO I'm talking about a banned organisation (by the way, don't you think Arafat's part of the organisation is becoming so respectable that even the Israeli government could talk to him?). If I show the colours and the flag of liberation I can be sent to gaol for five years. There is even a Palestinian artist who I know, who was sent to gaol for six months for using the black and green and red in a painting! As an Israeli, it's illegal for me to meet any one from the PLO – that's true for a Jew as well. How can I tell you about our lives? We were almost beaten to the ground in 1948, and in 1967 – but you mustn't think that other Arabs in the Middle East really support us. We are their pawns of international strategy and power games. Who cares about the Palestinian people? They can rot away into the ground of the refugee camps . . .

If I want to fight for my freedom and that of my people I must not get married: then I would be lost in that life of my children. But if I do not marry then the struggle is with my family first. My father is very strong in this, and he says it is not natural for a young woman to behave in my way. He wants to give money, to see me live in a smart house with the tall aerials that show I have a big television that gets the pictures from Saudi, from Jordan.

I will not do it. I will be one of the new Palestinian

women; I will show them. And when I leave home it will be
without the old uncle who is always supposed to travel with
me, to protect me. I do a lot of work with our women's
committee, to teach women to read (especially the older
ones), and to help them understand their life. Where are the
Palestinian women working? They are the worst paid of
anyone, in the fields and also the factories. They earn less
than the Arab men; the small factories pay them a lot less
than the bigger ones. So we will work with them as well.

I think that my freedom in my own life and what we all
want politically will be the same thing. If Hussein comes
back here to the West Bank [King Hussein of Jordan] how
will I be free? No, we have to have our own small State: that,
I think, is what the Jews are afraid of; they know it is no
good talking about Egypt looking after Gaza again, or
Jordan looking after us here. But we are not allowed to say
it, and while we sit in prison, or are sent into exile, their new
settlements take away more and more of our land. Perhaps
they think if they go on long enough we will just disappear?
They have already taken half our land since 1967. Will they
try to move a million people away from their homes? They
take our fields first, the houses go next.

There is a difficulty for Palestinian women. They know
that to have children makes their lives more difficult, but
they want to have them because they want to show the Jews
that they can live in this land, and be more not few in
number.

Our other difficulties are for everyone, not just the women.
We do not have books in our schools and many of our
villages do not have electricity. In my own village there are
no pipes, and the dirty water and other things run in the
open road. We were made to be poor when the land was
taken, and now we do not get the same money as a Jewish
town. We are so poor that the village council is owing
600 million shekels. Even the Bedouin villages are not so
poor, and they are more trusted by the government.

What does it help us, as Arabs in Israel, that we have the
vote? We are too few in number. You see, if the West Bank

and Gaza were properly joined to Israel, and all had that vote, then we would be nearly half of everybody. That is what the Jews are afraid of. But they do not want to have that kind of peace; and I don't think they want any other kind either. They keep talking about other Arabs who are not in the PLO for a conference. Who are these people? Who do they trust? It is not anyone that we have been asked about . . . and it is always a man.

If they want to talk, we will talk. We do not like guns, or terror. There is a real hate that grows and grows . . . when we lose our fields, we grow this hate instead. But I do believe we would talk, if they did really mean it. Even though I live in Israel, I know that it is in Gaza and the West Bank that the big answers will come. For that, I will live and do my work. And if I have to go to prison I will go.

Janet Aviad was born Janet O'Dea in the United States of America but – like many other new Israelis – she has taken a local surname. She has been one of the most active campaigners of the Peace Now campaign for many years.

I've been working for peace for many years. Peace Now started in 1978; the point of the movement is to influence Israeli public opinion towards a comprehensive peace in the region, towards achieving that as soon as possible. That means concession of all of the West Bank except for minor territorial changes on security grounds alone; recognition of the Palestinian right for a national determination or self-expression; trying to block whatever seem to be obstacles to the peace process such as settlements, Jewish terror, Jewish super-nationalism, chauvinism, racism, Kahanism – that's it.

I mean the main thing as a pressure group is to seize a national mood, a public mood, and channel it, move it in a certain direction. When no moves exist you can't do anything – this is the present moment: that's why activity is sporadic. The country is immersed in economic problems: everyone thinks of their pay cheque and no one cares about anything.

We've had ups and downs – a good demonstration for

Peace Now is 100,000. If that were translated in terms of the United States population it would mean four million taking to the streets: that's a good demo! We reached 400,000 in the protest against the razing of Sabra and Shatilla, which was gigantic, unique. I don't think the constituency we got there we'd get again readily: that brought together so many sectors of the population due to the really major discontent with the entire Lebanese adventure, plus the smell over Sabra and Shatilla. We seized the right moment and did everything correctly. That was a big climax to a summer of demonstrating.

The majority of the population is not Orthodox – and the Orthodox have not gained in number here. They are 25 per cent of the population: it's a significant minority.[1] Most people are defined as traditionalist; sometimes they support that minority and sometimes they don't. I'm not worried about a theocracy. I mean it's something we should fight and be aware of, but not something that seems to me to be around the corner.

I am very worried about fascist tendencies and ultra-nationalist tendencies, that's the fight we're engaged in now at Shalom Akschav, but I don't think we're losing it. In terms of media attention they're on the up but when it comes to real progress the settlements are actually frozen. In Israel, in the Middle East, things are very fluid; things change from one end to the other and you can never take one picture and say 'That's Israel'.

Judaism as a religion is not democratic. Neither is Christianity, neither is Islam. The Jewish God is not tolerant of various pluralistic options. He's a zealous God and he wants his chosen people – I mean according to religious interpretation – to behave in a certain way. There are different traditions within Judaism and it depends which has the ascendancy: there are ways of interpretation which allow it to be stretched. It can be more universalist and pluralist

---

1 In the Knesset, however, Orthodox Jews are very strong because they usually hold the balance of power under Israel's system of proportional representation.

and less violent and nationalistic. In fact Judaism can be violent or non-violent, depending on the period, the sociological and political factors. Judaism is an ocean and you can find the interpretation that suits you and your politics.

We have an internal war among the Rabbis in which the Orthodox Rabbis, mainly of the Right – of the non-democratic, non-liberal perspective – are on the one side and a minority of Rabbis are in the opposite camp. We'll fight it out, there's no determinism here.

Don't forget that it's a democratic State, more democratic than England: during the Lebanon war we were able to condemn the war and bring the soldier back from the front to talk about it and against it. I think during the Falklands they didn't even let anything be on the television . . . it's a democratic society and it's still liberal and open; at the same time the democracy *is* threatened – there are tensions and threats and it's a very difficult situation. Because of Arab terror we're always in a defensive posture, so you have to take the whole picture into account and not adopt the simplistic outlook that Israel is going into fascism. I reject that entirely. And I think that Judaism in Israel can be stretched, and be more liberal – and it will be again.

The West Bank – the situation *there* is creeping towards South Africa. Of course you don't have anything like Peace Now in South Africa . . . Jews fighting to defend the rights of the Palestinians and to get us out of the West Bank, because it's cancerous. Peace Now represents 30 per cent of the country on these issues all the time: those are a part of us and at other times another 20 per cent join us so that we represent half the country.

Over the Green Line you have this really bad situation of two peoples fighting for one land where one is the conqueror and one is the conquered. It's a colonial situation with all the negative, immoral manifestations of colonialism. What we try to do there is point out continually to the sane Israelis, the other Israelis, that's a contradiction of Zionism and of Judaism, this growing apartheid. On the West Bank there are

40,000 Jews living now who expropriate land, who block wells and build roads through other people's agricultural lands. They put the Palestinians under restrictions – I would say that the settlers in effect live through violence and their ultimate goal is to strangle the Palestinians so that they'll leave, but peacefully.

Many don't agree with Kahane; they don't want to throw them out like he does – they don't agree with Kahane, but in effect it's the same thing. And our goal is to make sure they can't do it their way either, by encouraging the peace process. I think, though, we are in bad shape, because I don't see anything happening. If there would be a move to either throw the Palestinians out or to annex the West Bank and Gaza you would have an entire movement against – a movement creating disruption and civil strife in Israel. But this way, this de facto annexation – the whole business has been deliberately fudged, by the Labour Party first and then the Likud; Labour is just as much to blame. It started settlements, encouraged settlements; never made up its mind and then finally advocated the Allon Plan,[2] which is unacceptable to the Palestinians.

Everyone's idea is to run away from decision-making – hard to make because of the real security problems. Instead of making a decision you sort of let the situation remain as it is, drag the thing out and hope that somehow it will take care of itself. That's what Labour did: not recognise the problems. Golda refused to recognise that there were Palestinians. That approach led to people ignoring it, trying not to see what happens over the Green Line. They don't visit, they don't know any Arabs, and they don't understand what's happening. Do they want to know? One of our jobs is to tell them.

2 Under the Allon Plan devised by a Labour government, Israel would have officially annexed a third of the West Bank and attempted to resolve the future of the rest of the territory. It is yet another example of official resolve that was never implemented; instead, under the uneasy guise of a military administration, half the land has gone. In Gaza, which is similarly governed, more than a third of the area now has Israeli settlers.

People born after 1967 don't know any other reality, and the maps make it look like it's all the same . . . when they interview a settler on radio he or she will say 'I'm from Karnesh Shomrona'; or 'I'm so-and-so from Ofra' – as if it's any other Jewish town with the same rights, the same everything; as though nothing is in question. We have to show what problems the settlements create for the country morally and economically, and politically in the world inside and outside . . . it's a very difficult situation.

If I say that I would like to travel to the West Bank with a visa, people think I'm out of my mind . . . I don't like to go to the West Bank or Gaza: I go only to demonstrate or have a meeting. I'd never go for pleasure – I feel like I'm a conqueror there. You go north or south of Jerusalem: the only sign that you're entering the West Bank is a security check. The Israelis don't have to stop because they are recognised by their different colour number plate . . . the Palestinians are stopped and checked and we just go through. Many Israelis never see an Arab, except as a hewer of wood and a drawer of water: in Israel that means as a collector of garbage and as building workers – they're engaged in those jobs, and that's the only contact.

It's another colonial situation, that's what it is. It wouldn't bother me at all if we lived within the pre-1967 boundaries as a more or less Jewish society, with a few contacts. In the Middle East, quite traditionally, peoples have lived alongside each other with some economic contact and very limited social ties . . . that's the privilege of the different peoples. I cannot bear subjecting another people and not allowing them – they're not free, they're not equal. And the same goes in part, but less so, for the Israeli Arab. The job has to be done of bettering the conditions of the Israeli Arab and of changing the situation on the West Bank to allow either a Palestinian State or some form of self-definition, whatever they decide.

I thought Ms Aviad's concern for both nations good and proper, except for her statement that most of the population was not Orthodox: it fell immediately into the same trap I had felt closing over my own head when I watched the Maccabee Games. Israel was being defined only by its Jewish inhabitants, whereas even the Proclamation of Independence of 1948 had spoken of equality of social and political rights for all its citizens, without distinction of creed, race or sex. I have been guilty of that bias too, on this journey, because there has been no even-handed treatment or analysis. Is it really possible to look at both sides at the same time? At least I had been continually aware that there was more than one story to tell. I had also found a unity between the personal and the political, spread right across differing groups, that had helped shape a coherent pattern of explanation and understanding.

The journey had been an illumination that the small, if comfortable, shifts towards a modicum of greater power for women in Britain during the past ten years had been possible only because a liberal democracy could afford them. In Israel, as on the West Bank, that was not feasible for a Jewish State that depended on enormous military strength to maintain an uneasy and brutalising status quo. It had made victims of the Palestinians (the victims of victims, Salman Rushdie said recently) and paradoxically was enabling militant Arab women to grow faster in their struggle for equality of opportunity and status than their Jewish colleagues. They were working for a multi-faceted liberation and the Jewish women, caught between homemaking, the demands of military supremacy and old-fashioned religious ideas, were being left rapidly behind.

I had personally trodden a cautious path in my determination to meet women of all colours and persuasions. That had meant ignoring most demonstrations and meetings as I moved from town to countryside, between Israel, the West Bank and Gaza, and from Right to Left. Perhaps the most surprising thing of all, during the travelling, was how difficult it was to penetrate the thick layers of unknowingness, the pretence people had that they didn't know what I was talking about. Many seemed wrapped in furs against the heat and anger spawned on all sides and in every argument. The talk about the future, so much a part of daily debate, had a more unreal tone on the Left. Those who were members of Gush Emunim, Likud or Tehiya not only knew where they wanted to go: they were already moving in that direction. And lying battered in their wake lay truth, civil liberty, the rule of law and equal rights for women.

INDEX

Abbadee, Achmed, 152
Abbass, Hiam, 75–7
Abdullah, 47
abortion, 19, 74, 140
Abuish, 95
Afula, 127, 128, 129
Alisa, 85
Allan, Michael, 76–7
Allenby Bridge, 35, 122
Allon, Second Lt. Dennis, 25–6
Allon Plan, 167 and n.
Aloni, Shulamit, 6
Alsaana, Sayyid, 92–4, 96
Amnesty International, 54
Andrianov, Amira, 99–103
anti-semitism, 139, 148
Arabs: attitude of Jews towards, 63,
 64, 127; discrimination against, 5,
 6, 36–40, 51, 53, 102, 127, 129,
 146, 151, 155 (see also racism);
 education, 5, 27, 56, 98, 108,
 114; employment, 3, 26, 85–6,
 89–92, 102, 149, 150, 168;
 expulsion, 7, 17 and n., 18, 22–3,
 47, 61, 163, 167; language, 48–9;
 not in army, 21, 48n. wages, 5,
 100–1, 151, 163; wars with see
 militarism; see also Muslims, Gaza;
 West Bank
Arafat, Y., 162

Arieli, Dana, 44–5
Arlosoroff, Chaim, 47 and n.
arms: guns, 12, 16, 21–2, 23, 45,
 122–3, 148, 150, 155; industry, 6,
 23, 149 and n.
army service, 2, 3, 5–6, 12–13, 21
 and n., 23, 85, 94, 105, 134; Arabs
 not in, 21, 48n.; checkpoints, 9, 36,
 168; Reserve duty, 32–3, 42;
 women in, 32, 34–51
Ashkenazi, 6, 11, 58, 59, 86–7, 88,
 149
Asla, 60
Athens, 60
Aviad, Janet, 164–8

Baqa Al Kirbaya, 128, 129
Barkai, Kibbutz, 127–43
Bedouin, 2, 6, 48, 74, 92–7, 163
Beersheva, 92, 95–7
Begin, M., 6, 7, 30, 115, 135
Beirut, 60
Ben Aharon, Rivka, 60–5
Ben Yehuda, Netiva, 9, 33 and n.,
 34–5, 56, 57, 70–1, 109–10, 111
Ben Zvi, Nitza, 84–5
Ben-Gurion, David, 6, 73 and n., 84,
 86, 102
Benvenisti, Dr Meron, 151
Berger, Shulamit, 53, 54

171